Hazards and Problems
Take Notice, Take Care

The author and the publishers stress that walkers should be aware of the dangers that may occur on all walks.

- check local weather forecast before walking; do not walk up into mist or low clouds
- use local OS maps side by side with walking guides
- wear walking boots and clothing
- do not take any unnecessary risks – conditions can change suddenly and can vary from season to season
- take special care when accompanied by children or dogs
- when walking on roads, ensure that you are conspicuous to traffic from either direction

Short Family Walks in Snowdonia

Dorothy Hamilton

ISBN: 978-1-84524-079-0

Cover design: Sian Parry

Published by
Llygad Gwalch, Ysgubor Plas, Llwyndyrys,
Pwllheli, Gwynedd LL53 6NG
☎ 01758 750432   🖷 01758 750438
✆ books@carreg-gwalch.com
Web site: www.carreg-gwalch.com

Dorothy Hamilton
Dorothy lives in Meirionnydd. She has written other walking guidebooks, including Circular Walks on Anglesey, Circular Walks Around Beddgelert, Walks from Welsh Heritage Railways and Walks from National Trust Properties (Central and Southern Wales). She is also a contributor to walking, history and countryside magazines. A keen walker, she has undertaken several long distance walks in Wales, Scotland, England, Ireland, Norway, France and other European countries.

Dedicated to my daughter Abigail

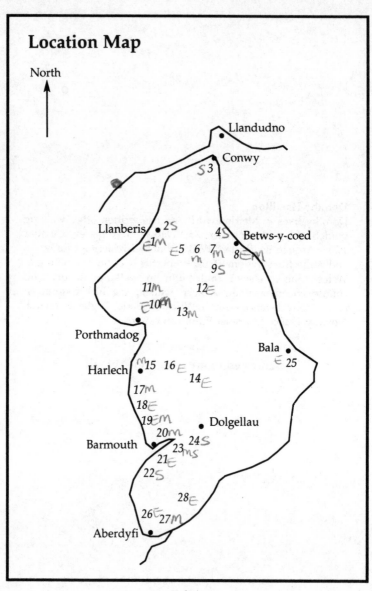

Location Map

North

Llandudno

Conwy

S 3

Llanberis
● 2S
1M
E
● 4S
Betws-y-coed
5 6 7 8
m M
EM
9S
11M 12E
10M 13M

Porthmadog
●

Bala
● 25
E

Harlech
● 15 16E
17M 14E
18E
19EM
20M
Dolgellau ●
24S
Barmouth
● 23MS
21E
22S
28E
26E 27M
Aberdyfi ●

Contents

Introduction

Snowdonia is known for its beautiful, mountain scenery and, whilst the best way to explore this stunning region is on foot, it is not necessary to climb the high mountains to enjoy this National Park`s varied landscape. This book of walks is written with families in mind, as well as individuals who do not wish to undertake long or arduous walks. They range from walks with options of under two miles to a maximum of five miles.

These circular walks feature viewpoints, lakes, waterfalls, riverbanks, woodlands and nature reserves. On some of the routes you will also encounter the ruins of castles, steam railways, prehistoric sites and other places of historical and legendary interest.

Readers will find a list of the walks provided in order of difficulty. Inexperienced walkers and those with young children are advised to do some of the walks at the top of the Easy list first. Times are not given for the walks as they can vary according to the family`s experience and the children`s ages. Generally speaking, children under seven years of age are unlikely to cover more than one mile per hour.

Many of the walks start and finish near refreshment places, but it is also advisable to carry food and drinks for short breaks and picnics. Footwear should be sturdy with good grip on the soles. If in doubt about the weather, carry waterproofs. Do not hesitate to turn back or take a short option if the weather worsens and you are less than halfway through the walk.

Children of all ages can help with the navigation of the walks by looking out for stiles, waymarks, signposts and landscape features. It is a good idea to carry a simple field guide for identifying the flowers, trees, butterflies, birds and other wildlife that you see on your walks. Allow time for play at picnic places. Happy walking!

Welsh Place Names

The following words are frequently used in the names of places in Wales. They may be followed by the name of a saint or a topographical feature such as a river. Look out for them on signs and maps.

Aber – *estuary, river mouth*
Afon – *river*
Allt/Gallt – *hill, slope*
Bach/Fach – *small*
Bedd – *grave, tomb*
Bryn – *hill*
Bwlch – *pass*
Cadair/Gadair – *chair*
Cae – *field*
Caer/Gaer – *fort*
Canol – *middle, centre*
Capel – *chapel*
Carn – *cairn*
Carreg – *rock, stone*
Castell – *castle*
Cefn – *ridge*
Coch – *red*
Coed – *wood, trees*
Craig – *rock*
Croes – *cross*
Cwm – *valley*
Dinas – *fort*
Dol/Ddol – *meadow*
Du/Ddu – *black*
Dwr – *water*
Dyffryn – *valley*

Eglwys – *church*
Ffordd – *road*
Ffridd – *mountain pasture*
Ffynnon – *spring, well*
Glan – *riverbank*
Glas – *blue*
Golau – *light*
Gorsaf – *station*
Gwyn – *white*
Hafod/Hafoty – *summer dwelling*
Hen – *old*
Hendre – *winter dwelling*
Heol – *road*
Isaf – *lower*
Lon – *lane*
Llan – *church*
Llety – *lodging*
Llwybr – *path*
Llyn – *lake*
Llys – *court, palace*
Maen – *stone*
Maes – *field*
Melin/Felin – *mill*
Mawr/Fawr – *big, great*
Mor – *sea*
Morfa – *marsh*
Muriau – *walls*
Mynydd/Fynydd – *mountain*
Nant – stream, *ravine*
Neuadd – *hall*
Newydd – *new*
Pandy – *fulling-mill*
Pant – *hollow, valley*
Parc – *park, field*

Pen – *head, top*
Penrhyn – *promontory, headland*
Pentre – *village*
Pistyll – *spout, cataract*
Plas – *mansion*
Pont – *bridge*
Porth – *port*
Pwll – *pool*
Rhaeadr – *cataract, waterfall*
Rhyd – *ford*
Sarn – *causeway, road*
Tafarn – *inn*
Tan – *under*
Traeth – *beach*
Tre/Tref – *town*
Ty – *house*
Uchaf – *upper*
Y/Yr – *the*
Ynys – *island*

Walks in Order of Difficulty

These lists are provided to help families with young children, as well as other people new to walking, decide which walks to choose. The walks have been graded with families in mind and none of the walks would be considered strenuous by experienced walkers. Families with very young children and individuals with little experience are advised to do some of the walks near the top of the Easy list first.

Easy Walks – level or with short or easy uphill sections

Walk 10   Beddgelert 1 and a half miles (short route)
Walk 25   Bala 2 miles
Walk 21   Morfa Mawddach 2 miles
Walk 12   Dolwyddelan 2 miles
Walk 14   Coed y Brenin 2 and a quarter miles
Walk 16   Harlech 1 and a half miles (short route)
Walk 19   Talybont 1 and a quarter miles (short route)
Walk 5   Llyn Crafnant 3 and a half miles
Walk 26   Tywyn 4 and a half miles
Walk 8   Betws-y-coed (Miner`s Bridge) 2 miles (short route)
Walk 1   Llanberis (Castle) 2 and a half miles (short route)
Walk 18   Dyffryn Ardudwy 2 and a half miles
Walk 28   Llanfihangel-y-pennant 3 and a half miles

Moderate Walks

Walk 6   Llyn Geirionydd 2 miles
Walk 13   Llyn Mair 3 miles
Walk 10   Beddgelert 3 miles (long route)

More Strenuous Walks

Tourist Information Centres

Aberdyfi	01654 767321
Bala	01678 521021
Barmouth	01341 280787
Betws-y-coed	01690 710426
Conwy	01492 592248
Dolgellau	01341 422888
Harlech	01766 780658
Llanberis	01286 870765
Porthmadog	01766 512981
Tywyn	01654 710070

The Country Code

Plan ahead.
Keep to the public rights of way across farmland.
Leave farm gates as you find them.
Keep dogs under close control.
Carry your litter home.
Protect all wildlife, plants and trees.
Consider other people.

2.5 or 3 miles (4 or 5 kilometres)

Llanberis – Dolbadarn Castle and Waterfall

Route: After visiting Dolbadarn Castle, the walk climbs through woods to a great viewpoint, where there is a café. You have the option of seeing Ceunant Mawr Falls (another short climb) before returning along the shores of Llyn Padarn.

Start: Car park on road to Llyn Padarn Country Park, opposite Dolbararn Castle.

Access: Llanberis is on the A4086, south-east of Caernarfon. Car park signposted.Buses from Caernarfon and Bangor.

Facilities: Cafes and public toilets on the route. Full facilities in Llanberis. Two children`s playgrounds on the walk.

Maps: Ordnance Survey Explorer OL17; Landrangrer 115.

The remains of Dolbadarn Castle with its tall keep stands on a rocky knoll above Llyn Peris. It was built in the early 13th century by Llywelyn ap Iorwerth (the Great) to guard the route through the mountains. It is said that Llywelyn ap Gruffudd imprisoned his brother Owain here. It is also believed that during the 15th century, Owain Glyndwr`s enemy Lord Grey of Ruthin was held captured in the castle.

From the castle are views over Llyn Peris and Llyn Padarn. Llyn Peris is the lower lake for the Dinorwic Power Station. Water from the upper lake, Llyn Marclyn Mawr, flows through tunnels, generating electricity, in

Walk 1
Llanberis

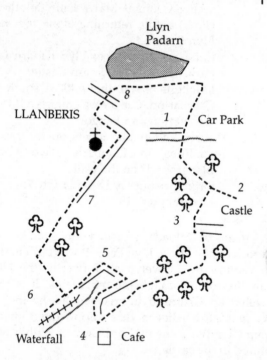

North

Llyn Padarn

LLANBERIS

8

1   Car Park

2   Castle

3

7

5

6

Waterfall   4   ☐ Cafe

the mountain Elidir Fawr. The water is then stored in Llyn Peris until low peak times when it is pumped back to the high mountain lake.

Walk directions:

1. From the car park, go out to the road and cross it to a footpath. Cross a footbridge and follow a path uphill through the trees to Dolbadarn Castle.

2. After visiting the castle, go back through the kissing-gate and pass a small building then turn left on a path to have a wall on the left. Ignore a path on the right and, further on, go left on a path beside a fence. Go through a kissing-gate and walk beside a left-hand fence to a gate and road.

3. Cross the road with care and go left a few paces to a ladder stile. Follow the winding track through the woods. It passes through a kissing-gate and, higher up, you will have views of Llyn Padarn. Go through another kissing-gate and pass below a house to another gate. Here you may like to take refreshments at Pen y Ceunant Isaf Tea Garden and Café.

4. From the café, turn right downhill along a lane and go through a small gate at a cattle grid. Soon go left on a road that passes under the Snowdon Mountain Railway viaduct and passes a children's playground on the right. Ignore a road on the right and, after a few paces, if you want to see the waterfall, turn left through a gate at a cattle grid. (If you are not going to the waterfall, continue along the road and skip all directions until point 7).

5. Walk uphill along the lane and, after about 250 metres, you will pass a footpath and houses on the right. After a

few more paces, go left, taking care as you cross the Snowdon Mountain Railway track, to a viewpoint of Ceunant Mawr Waterfall.

6. Walk back along the lane for a short distance, then go left along a footpath. Join a track and turn left for about 40 metres, then turn right on a path. It crosses a stream and goes through a kissing-gate. Follow the clear, stony path downhill, passing a house on the right. Go through a kissing-gate and down steps to a lane. Turn left, rejoining the shorter route.

7. Pass St Padarn's Church, and turn left along a road for about 150 metres. Bear right at a signpost and pass public toilets on the left. Cross the road to Llyn Padarn, where there is a children's playground. Turn right and cross a small footbridge then follow a path beside the lake, passing picnic tables.

8. Go through a gate into Llyn Padarn Country Park. Follow the path through a kissing-gate and pass a small belt of trees. On reaching a broad level footbridge (cross it and turn left if you wish to visit the Slate Museum) turn right and follow a path to the car park at the start of the walk.

Llanberis − Circuit of Llyn Padarn

Route: This varied walk on woodland paths, tracks and lanes takes you around Llyn Padarn and has great viewpoints along the way. Some climbing at the start, otherwise downhill and level walking.

Start: Padarn Country Park car park near the Slate Museum.

Access: Llanberis is on the A4086, south-east of Caernarfon. The country park and car park are signposted. Buses from Bangor and Caernarfon to Llanberis.

Facilities: Many attractions in Padarn Country Park, including the Slate Museum, where there is a café. Public toilets in the car park and on the route. Picnic tables and benches on the walk at viewpoints. Children`s playground near the end of the walk.

Maps: Ordnance Survey Explorer OL17; Landranger 115.

Llanberis lies at the foot of Snowdon and, on a clear day, you can enjoy superb views of this majestic mountain on the walk. Padarn Country Park is located on the site of the Dinorwig quarry which operated from 1787 to 1969. In the Slate Museum you can learn about the slate mining industry and see typical quarrymen`s cottages and the largest waterwheel in Wales.

The walk passes the Quarry Hospital, now a museum, where injured workers were treated. The route then

Walk 2
Llanberis

North

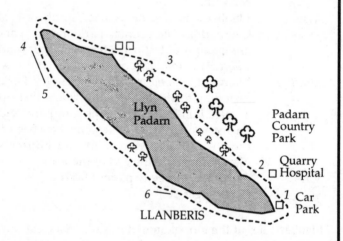

Llyn Padarn

Padarn Country Park

Quarry Hospital

1 Car Park

2

3

4

5

6

LLANBERIS

passes through woodlands where flowers such as bluebells and wood sorrel may be seen in the spring. There are several viewpoints of the lake and Snowdon. The lake is home to the rare artic char and it is a Site of Special Scientific Interest.

On the other side of Llyn Padarn, the walk follows the trackbed of the former Llanberis to Caernarfon railway line which opened in 1869. The passenger service stopped in 1930 and the line closed completely in 1964. It is now a cycleway as well as a walking trail.

Walk directions:

1. At the car park, have the lake railway on your right and walk towards the notice board with a large white arrow for the Quarry Hospital. Follow a wide path and soon go right on a path marked with different colours. It goes over a bridge and uphill to a viewpoint of the lake and mountains. Cross a bridge over the railway and climb steps to the Quarry Hospital.

2. Pass the hospital on your right and go through a gate into the wood. Follow the path past an old building to a viewpoint and bench. Ignore a path on the right and continue with the lake below on your left. After another viewpoint, the path descends slightly. Ignore a path on the left and walk downhill to a gate and leave the Country Park. Cross a bridge and walk uphill on a track. Ignore a kissing-gate on the right and pass a quarry and Cwm Derwen. Continue uphill and, at a right bend, leave the track to take a path to steps and a lane.

3. Turn left and walk downhill, passing houses at Fachwen. Further on, the lake is nearby on your left. Pass a viewpoint and walk across a bridge at the end of the

lake. Turn left to climb a stile at a broad gate. Continue along an old road with the lake on your left. At a bend there is a plaque on a rock on the right commemorating the Centenary of the North Wales Quarrymen's Union. Reach a ladder stile at fields and continue to another stile and bridle gate.

4. Turn left along the pavement for about 200 metres then, at a post with a white band, go left on a railed path downhill to a wide track. Bear left along Lon Peris Walking/Cycling Trail. The lake is nearby on your left.

5. The track passes through trees and you will see a pool on your right. Pass an inlet of the lake and walk around a barrier. At toilets on the right, go left, then quickly right on a path near a car park. Walk through trees to another car park and pass it on your left then cross to another stretch of path. Follow it to a road and turn left along the pavement.

6. On reaching the main road, turn left along the wide pavement to the village car park. Here go left on a path beside the lake, passing the car park on your right. Continue on the path beside the lake and pass a children's playground. Cross a small footbridge beside the lake and pass picnic tables. Go through a gate into Padarn Country Park and continue through a kissing-gate and past some trees. Follow wooden posts to a broad footbridge and cross it then turn left to the car park at the start.

4.5 miles/7.2 kilometres

Conwy

Route:	This superb walk rises gradually to the ridge of Conwy Mountain, from where you can enjoy superb views.
Start:	Lancaster Square, Conwy.
Access:	Conwy is on the A547. Car parks, railway station and bus stop near the start. Buses from Llandudno, Bangor, Llanrwst and other towns call at Conwy.
Facilities:	Cafes, pubs, public toilets and other facilities in Conwy.
Maps:	Ordnance Survey Explorer OL17; Landranger 115.

The history of the town of Conwy goes back to the 12th century when the abbey of Aberconwy was built on the site of the present parish church. Llywelyn ap Iorwerth (the Great) , whose statue is in Lancaster Square, granted the charter for the abbey and he became a monk before he died. He was buried at Aberconwy. When Edward 1 started his programme of building castles to suppress the Welsh, the abbey was moved to Maenan up the river and Llywelyn`s coffin was taken there. The castle took four years to build and Welsh people were not allowed to live in the town. Owain Glyndwr`s followers captured the castle in 1401 and held it for two months.

On the walk you climb to the ridge of Conwy Mountain where you can enjoy great views over Conwy Bay to the Great Orme (Y Gogarth) and Llandudno. On the summit are the remains of an Iron Age hill fort with

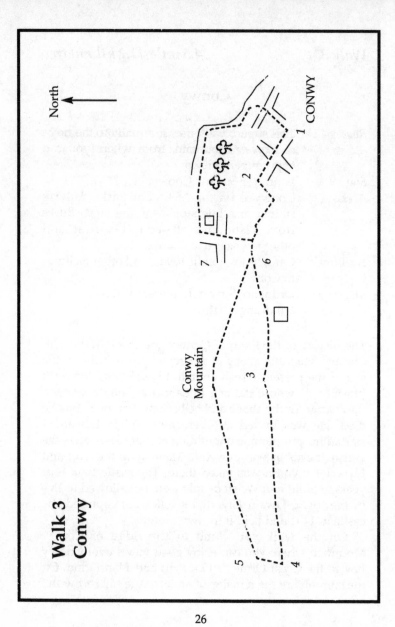

**Walk 3
Conwy**

North

Conwy Mountain

CONWY

1

2

3

4

5

6

7

the remains of about fifty round huts and house platforms.

On your way back through the town you will pass several historic houses that can be visited, including Aberconwy House, a three storey medieval house, and Plas Mawr. Plas Mawr was built in the 16th century by Robert Wynn of Gwydir Castle near Llanrwst. It is possible to walk around some sections of the town walls.

Walk directions:

1. Leave the square by having it on your right and following the one-way road uphill, passing the Police Station on your right. Go through the arch in the town wall and go over a crossroads. Maintain your direction for about 100 metres then turn left into Cadnant Park.

2. Cross a bridge over the railway line and bear right. Ignore the first road on the left and, further on, veer left with the road. After a few more metres, go right along Mountain Road. Ignore a road on the right and bear left to a fork. Take the left-hand track and ignore a stile on the right. On reaching gates near a house, take the right-hand gate and continue along a shady track. You will soon have a wall on your left.

3. Cross over another track to maintain your direction along a path. It climbs gradually with open views on the left and Conwy Mountain on our right. Ignore a path with a white arrow on the right and pass an erosion control area. Have a wall on your left and ignore a path on the right.

4. Just before the track descends to a dip, go right on a narrow path that climbs towards a rock. Pass the rock and reach a junction of paths. Ignore a path on the left and a

narrow path on the right. Take the second path on the right that rises slightly following the direction of an arrow waymark. Walk uphill and, after about 50 metres, you will reach a superb viewpoint. Turn right and, when a path joins from the left, keep to the right. Continue along a broad path, ignoring paths off. Just before reaching the ridge of Conwy Mountain, the path veers to the right then swings left.

5. Climb to the ridge and pass an information plaque about Conwy Mountain Hill Fort. Walk through the fort and continue along the ridge with great views of Conwy Bay and the town of Conwy. Descend a short steep section and continue along the main path. When a small hump is in front of you, follow the good path on the left that goes around the hill to a path junction. Ignore the path on the right and go left on a path with a waymark. It descends gradually along the side of the hill to a ladder stile.

6. Bear left, soon passing the track used earlier. Walk down the lane but, when the lane bends right, instead of retracing your steps, go left along a narrow lane which becomes a track. Cross a footbridge over the railway line to emerge on the main road.

7. Cross at the traffic lights and bear right then left along Morfa Drive. Pass Aberconwy School on your right and walk along the right-hand pavement to follow a wall that curves to the right. Join a broad path and you will soon have a wood on your right and Conwy Estuary on your left. The path joins a road where you turn left through an arch in the wall. Pass the Smallest House in Britain and, after the Liverpool Arms, go right through the Lower Gate. Cross a road at traffic lights and walk uphill to the square at the start.

Trefriw – Waterfalls and Llanrhychwyn Church

Route: This walk takes you to a viewpoint of
            Trefriw`s Fairy Falls before climbing through
            woodlands to a fine viewpoint above the
            Crafnant Valley. The route then continues to
            the medieval Llanrhychwyn Church before
            returning along paths and lanes.

Start: Car park in Trefriw village.

Access: Trefriw is on the B5106 on the west side of
            the Conwy Valley. Buses from Llangollen,
            Llandudno and Conwy pass through
            Trefriw.

Facilities: Cafes, pubs and shops in Trefriw. Public
            toilets near the car park.
            Children`s playground near the far end of
            the car park.

Maps: Ordnance Survey OL17; Landranger 115.

Trefriw was a flourishing inland port in the 19th century
when slate, lead ore and timber were shipped along the
river for export. Many visitors travelled by paddle
steamer from Llandudno and Conwy to take the sulphur
and iron rich waters from the spa north of the village. The
passenger steamer service continued until the Second
World War. The woollen mill was originally a fulling mill
(pandy) where cloth woven by local cottagers was
washed and finished.

After visiting the waterfalls, the walk climbs through
woodlands to a fine viewpoint over Cwm Crafnant. From
here you can see the ruin of Klondike Mill where lead ore

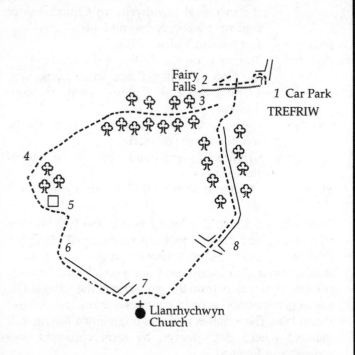

Walk 4
Trefriw

North

Fairy
Falls 2

1 Car Park
TREFRIW

3

4

5

6

7

Llanrhychwyn
Church

8

30

and zinc ore from the Pandora Mine near Llyn Geirionydd were processed. Further on you can visit Llanrhychwyn Church, thought to be one of the oldest in Wales. Dating from the 12th century, it is dedicated to St Rhychwyn, a sixth century Celtic saint. It is said that Llywelyn ap Iorwerth (the Great) and his wife Siwan (Joan), the illegitimate daughter of King John, used to worship at this medieval church. Because Siwan found the climb tiring, a church was built for her in the valley at the place that is now Trefriw.

Walk directions:

1. From the car park walk out to the main road and turn right over the bridge. Take the first road on the left and walk uphill. Soon go left on an enclosed path to Afon Crafnant. Ignore a bridge and walk beside the river, passing through a kissing-gate. Pass the lower falls and continue to a view of the upper falls where there is an information board.

2. The path veers right to a kissing-gate. Cross the footbridge and then go right on a path, with the river on your right. Emerge on a road and turn right to another road. Turn left and, after about 80 metres, go right on a path into woodland.

3. Follow the main path and climb a stile. The path you are following levels out for a while as it passes through the woods then descends a little before crossing a bracken covered hillside with open views. It climbs into trees again and reaches a rocky viewpoint. Ahead in the valley is the Klondike Mill.

4. Pass another viewpoint and continue through trees. Just before reaching a wall, bear left on a narrow path.

Walk uphill beside a right-hand wall. The path bears right through a gap in a wall, then goes uphill to a stile. Pass a house on the left and go through a gate and walk along a drive.

5. After about 100 metres, you reach a fork. Turn right and before reaching a house, go left on a track. At buildings, bear right for a few paces then go left on a track bordered by tall trees. Emerge through a gate onto a lane.

6. Turn left along the lane and go through a gate across it. Pass farm buildings on the left and walk downhill. At a left bend, bear right on an access lane and, when it bends sharp right, go left through a partly hidden kissing-gate. After a few paces, you will reach the lych-gate of Llanrhychwyn Church.

7. Continue along the right-hand fence and go through a kissing-gate. Walk downhill, passing through two more kissing-gates then down steps to emerge on a track near a house. Turn left along the track to a lane.

8. Cross over the lane to another signed Trefriw. Follow it downhill, passing through woodlands and with views of the Conwy Valley below on your right. At a house on the left, ignore a footpath on the right and continue along the lane for another 100 metres then go right on a path to a road. Turn left and cross over another road to an enclosed path. Follow it to the footbridge over the river and retrace your steps to the start of the walk.

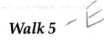
Llyn Crafnant

Route: This is an almost level, easy walk following tracks and a lane beside the beautiful lake Llyn Crafnant. There is one short section of rough path where the route leaves the forest track.

Start: Forestry Car park beside the lane about 200 metres before Llyn Crafnant.

Access: The lane to Llyn Crafnant starts in Trefriw on the B5106 in the Conwy Valley.

Facilities: Café and lakeside tea garden on the route. Toilets and picnic tables in the car park.

Maps: Ordnance Survey Explorer OL17; Landranger 115.

Llyn Crafnant is set in a beautiful, enclosed valley and it is popular with walkers. Near its outflow is a monument commemorating the gift of the lake in 1895 by Richard Jones as a water supply to the people of Llanrwst. The lake contains trout and is visited by birds such as mallards and mergansers. The Cynlloed farmhouse was used as a meeting place for non-conformists in the 19th century and, for a time, it was used as a Sunday School. Opposite the car park, a track leads to the Clogwyn y Fuwch slate quarry. Mainly consisting of underground workings, it closed in the early 20th century.

Walk 5
Llyn Crafnant

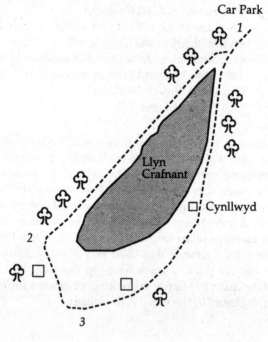

North

Car Park

Llyn
Crafnant

Cynllwyd

Walk directions:

1. From the car park, walk out to the lane and turn right. On reaching the lake, go right over a flat bridge and through a gate. Follow a track above the lake to a fork and turn left. The track passes above a stream and passes the end of the lake. Ignore a stile on the left. Follow the track as it goes downhill then rises to a waymarked post.

2. Go left on a path downhill to a ladder stile. Continue on the clear path downhill through woods and cross a footbridge near a house. Turn left on a track and go through a gate. Ignore a track to a house on the right and follow the main track downhill through meadows.

3. Turn left through a gate onto a lane and follow it, passing houses. In places there are superb views of Llyn Crafnant. Pass the Lakeside Café at Cynllwyd Mawr and follow the lane past the end of the lake to the start at the car park.

Llyn Geirionydd

Route:	Woodland and lakeside paths, tracks and lane. The path beside the lake is rough in places with tree roots across it and a slight scramble over a low, rocky promontory. Walkers can visit the Taliesin Monument which stands at the end of the lake.
Start:	Car park beside lane on the eastern side of Llyn Geirionydd.
Access:	Llyn Geirionydd can be reached by a lane starting at Tŷ Hyll *(the Ugly House)* on the A5 between Capel Curig and Betws-y-coed. Also by lane from the B5106 at Trefriw and west of Llanrwst.
Facilities:	Picnic tables and toilets at the car park. Several places beside the lake are ideal for picnics.
Maps:	Ordnance Survey Explorer OL17; Landranger 115.

Llyn Geirionydd is an attractive lake lying six hundred feet above sea level and between forested hills. Lead mining once took place in the area. On a small hill at the end of the lake stands a monument to the poet Taliesin who lived in the sixth century and it is said he lived near the lake. According to one legend he was found as a baby in a basket near the mouth of Afon Dyfi. The monument was erected in the early 19th century by the Ancaster family and later that century it was the custom to hold a yearly eisteddfod on the shores of the lake. It was

Walk 6
Llyn Geirionydd

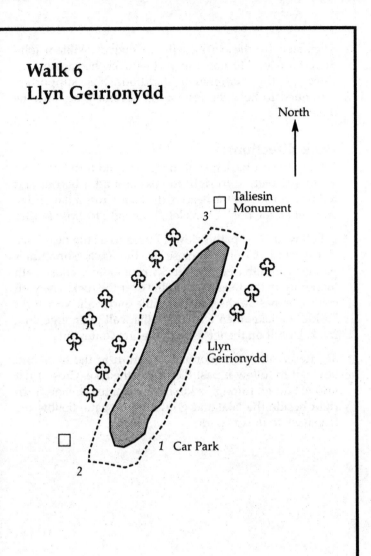

North

Taliesin
Monument

3

Llyn
Geirionydd

1 Car Park

2

originated by the bard Gwilym Cowlyd (William John Roberts), a local printer and poet who rebelled against the rules of the National Eisteddfod. His supporters continued to hold the festival for several years after he died in 1904.

Walk directions:

1. From the car park go out to the lane and turn left. After about 100 metres go right to pass around a barrier and follow a track past the head of the lake. Cross a flat bridge and, when the track bends left, bear right to cross a stile.

2. Follow a clear path below a house to a stile near Llyn Geirionydd. Continue close to the lake, sometimes passing through trees. At a rocky promontory take a path higher up in the trees to scramble over the rock. The path continues beside the lake to a stile and wall. Veer right beside the lake, then left beside the wall to emerge on a track. Uphill on the left is the Taliesin Monument.

3. After visiting the monument, return to the track and bear left to follow it past the end of the lake. Cross a flat bridge and go through a kissing-gate onto the lane. Turn right beside the lake and go through a gate. Follow the lane back to the car park.

Llyn Sarnau

Route: This walk visits the workings of old lead
              mines and then follows a scenic, undulating
              route along forest tracks and footpaths,
              passing another old lead mine before
              returning to the start.

Start: Llyn Sarnau car park.

Access: Leave the A5 at Tŷ Hyll *(the Ugly House)* by
              taking a lane uphill. Ignore a lane on the left
              after two miles and continue for half a mile
              to the car park, which is on your right. Llyn
              Sarnau can also be approached from the
              north-east by a lane leaving the B5106 south-
              west of Llanrwst.

Facilities: Picnic tables at the car park.

Maps: Ordnance Survey Explorer
              OL17; Landranger 115.

Llyn Sarnau is divided by a causeway and the lake is
usually dry during the summer months. It was created in
the 19th century to provide water for the nearby lead
mines. This walk takes you past the Llanrwst lead mine
and its tall chimney which is over fifty feet high. The
mine operated in the late 19th century and you can see
the remains of its engine house. The walk also passes the
Cyffty lead mine where you can see a wheelpit which
housed an enormous waterwheel. There are
interpretation boards at both sites. Along much of walk
are great views of Snowdonia's mountains.

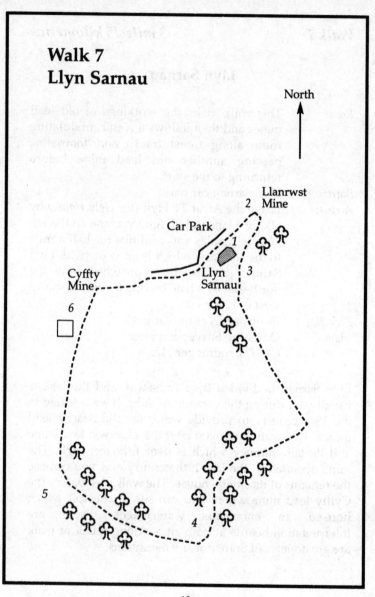

Walk 7
Llyn Sarnau

North

Llanrwst
Mine

Car Park

Cyffty
Mine

Llyn
Sarnau

6

5

4

3

2

1

Walk directions:

1. Walk out of the car park entrance and immediately turn right along a track. After about 80 metres, climb a stile on the left. Follow the fence and, at a gate on the left, bear right along a track for about 20 metres then go left on a path in the direction of the Llanrwst Mine`s tall chimney.

2. Pass the fence of the engine house and the chimney on your left and follow a path with a yellow arrow. It bears right to a ladder stile. Turn right on a track and pass around a barrier. Take a track on the left and follow it until you join another track. Turn right to a broad track.

3. Turn left along the track. Further on, trees have been felled opening up wide views.When the track divides, take a lesser track on the right. Ignore a footpath on the left and continue along the track, passing mine workings and a marshy area. Ignore a track on the right and continue to a corner wall and grassland on the right.

4. Walk on a few metres then bear right over a stile. Do not follow the left-hand fence that leads to a stile, but veer right on a grassy track and walk downhill. You will soon have a fence on the left. Climb a stile at a gate and follow a track through the forest. A bike trail comes in from the right. Continue along the track for about 50 metres then go right to climb a ladder stile next to a broad gate.

5. After a few metres, cross a ladder stile on your right and head uphill, parallel to the right-hand boundary. On reaching a grassy track, bear right to a stile at a gap. After passing it, go left uphill towards a marker post on a rock then veer slightly right to pass a building and a house.

6. Follow the track to a gate and ladder stile. Soon leave the track to go left to another stile in the far left bottom

corner. Go ahead to the next stile then walk uphill. You can take a path on the left to view the workings of the Cyffty Mine. Afterwards, continue uphill to a track below the lane. Turn right to more mine workings and go uphill to an information board. Join the lane and turn right to the start of the walk at the car park.

Betws-y-coed – Miner`s Bridge and Artists` Wood

Route:	This walk follows Afon Llugwy to the famous Miner`s Bridge. From here you can walk back along a lane or continue along the other side of the river then return through the forest known as Artists` Wood.
Start:	Railway Station entrance in Betws-y-coed. Car parks nearby and at Pont y Pair.
Access:	Betws-y-coed is on the A5. Trains from Llandudno and Blaenau Ffestiniog. Buses from Porthmadog, Blaenau Ffestiniog, Llangollen and Llandudno.
Facilities:	Shops, cafes and pubs in Betws-y-coed. Public toilets near the A5 and in Pont y Pair car park.
Maps:	Ordnance Survey Explorer OL17; Landranger 115.

The beautiful landscape surrounding Betws-y-coed has attracted visitors since the early years of the 19th century when Thomas Telford built the Waterloo Bridge and the London to Holyhead road. This walk follows the picturesque Afon Llugwy to the well known Miner`s Bridge. The original bridge was built as a short cut for miners living at Pentre Du across the river who worked at lead mines on the plateau to the north.

The longer walk crosses the bridge and continues through woodlands on the opposite of the river for nearly

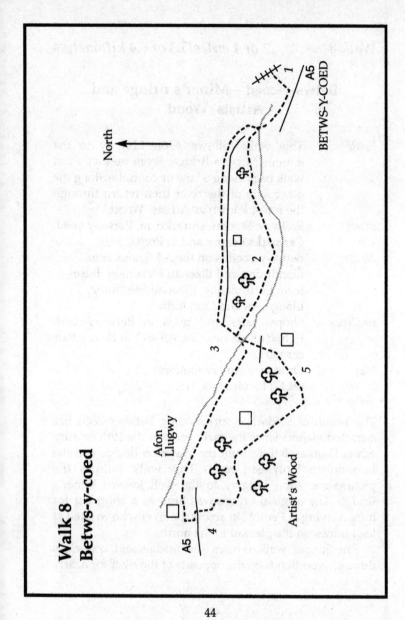

Walk 8
Betws-y-coed

North

BETWS-Y-COED

A5

1

2

3

A5

4

5

Afon Lliugwy

Artist's Wood

a mile. The route then returns through Artists` Wood with its broad leaved and coniferous trees. In the 19th century, many artists, including David Cox and Gastineau, used to visit Betws-y-coed and often painted in the vicinity of the wood. You will pass a stone that commemorates the planting of the first one hundred thousand acres of forest in North Wales by the Forestry Commission.

Walk directions

1. Have your back to the railway station entrance and turn left to the A5. Turn right and cross Pont y Pair over Afon Llugwy. Bear left and leave the lane to take a path beside the river and, at the end of the trees, climb a stile and follow the riverside path through a meadow.

2. Climb another stile into trees and continue on a path until you each the Miner`s Bridge. (For the short walk, do not cross it but go right uphill to a lane and turn right to Pont y Pair where you retrace your steps to the start.)

3. For the longer route, descend the Miner`s Bridge to the opposite side of the river and go up steps. Turn right into the trees to meet another path then turn right to have the river below on your right. There are good views of the gorge below. The path descends to the riverbank but soon climbs again. It crosses a footbridge over a stream and climbs over a little rock near the river. Stay on the main path and, after passing old mine buildings, go left to the road.

4. Turn left for a few metres then turn right on a forest track with the name Maesnewyddion. After about 30 metres, go left on a narrow path. It soon curves to the right and goes uphill to join another path. Turn left and, after about 50 metres, the path descends then rises beside

a fence which it follows around a corner. The path then goes downhill to cross a wooden footbridge near the road. Continue on the path, passing the commemoration stone on your right. After crossing a tiny footbridge, the path passes behind a house and, further on, goes through tall trees before emerging on a track.

5. Turn left downhill and pass a parking area. The track becomes surfaced and passes houses. Bear left to cross the A5 to a footpath leading to the Miner's Bridge. Here you can retrace your steps to the start or, after crossing the bridge, go uphill to a lane then turn right to Pont y Pair.

Betws-y-coed - Llyn Elsi

Route:	This walk follows a little known route to the popular, upland forest enclosed lake, Llyn Elsi. It then returns along paths and forest tracks.
Start:	Railway station entrance in Betws-y-coed. Car parks nearby.
Access:	Betws-y-coed is on the A5. Trains from Llandudno and Blaenau Ffestiniog. Buses from Porthmadog, Blaenau Ffestiniog, Llangollen and Llandudno.
Facilities:	Shops, cafes and pubs in Betws-y-coed. Public toilets near the A5.
Maps:	Ordnance Survey Explorer OL17; Landranger 115.

Surrounded by forest, Llyn Elsi is a pretty lake with small islets where black headed gulls bred. This walk takes you to a viewpoint above the lake from where you can enjoy superb views of Moel Siabod, the Glyder ridge and Carneddau mountains. It is a great spot for a picnic on a fine day. The monument on the hill commemorates the opening of a water supply from the lake to Betws-y-coed.

Walk directions:

1. Have your back to the railway station entrance and turn left to the A5. Turn right and ignore Pont y Pair on your right. You will soon have views of fields and Afon Llugwy on your right. Look out for a pub and guest houses on your left.

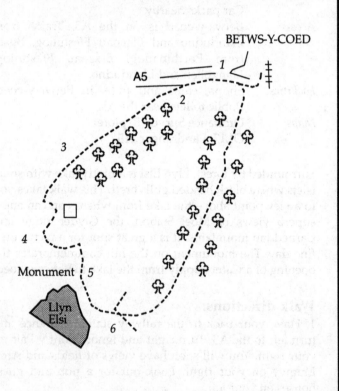

Walk 9
Betws-y-coed

North

BETWS-Y-COED

A5

1

2

3

4

Monument

5

Llyn
Elsi

6

2. Immediately after the last guest house (Dolgethin Guest House), and before a field on the left, go left on a track. Pass around a barrier and follow the track. It soon veers right and becomes narrower. Walk gradually uphill and, at a left bend, leave the track to cross a stile on the right next to a gate.

3. Go ahead on a stony track. Higher up you will see a field with ruins on the left and an old tramway and ruin on the right. Continue beside a wall. The path soon makes a sharp left turn to pass above a fenced quarry on the right. Climb a stile at a gate and continue on the path to have great views over the valley. Before reaching a barn, cross a stile on the right and veer right to follow the fence uphill along an old track marked with white arrows. Higher up, a wall curves in from the left. Have it on your left and go through a gap to continue with it on your right.

4. Emerge on a track and turn left along it. Climb a ladder stile to follow a path alongside a left-hand wall. Emerge on a forest track and turn left to walk around a barrier. Walk uphill until the track bends right and, soon afterwards, bear right on a clear path and follow it to the monument above Llyn Elsi.

5. Ignore a path on the left and one on the right and walk down the steep hill on a path that heads towards the lake. You will soon have the lake on your right. Walk beside it until you emerge on a forest track. Turn left and, at a fork, bear right.

6. Ignore a track on the right and walk downhill. Lower down, ignore a track on the left and a lesser track on the right. The track now veers to the left with views of the Conwy valley below. Ignore another track on the right

and paths leading off. You will soon pass a bench on the left. After passing around a barrier, go ahead to the A5 where you retrace your steps to the start.

Beddgelert

Route:	This lovely walk takes you along Afon Glaslyn as far as the Welsh Highland Railway's bridge, then returns along the other side of the river where there are suitable places for picnics. After viewing Gelert's Grave, you can choose to return to the village or follow a longer route offering superb views of the valley and surrounding mountains.
Start:	Beddgelert village car park on the A498.
Access:	Beddgelert lies north-east of Porthmadog and can be reached by the 4085 from Caernarfon or by leaving the A5 at Capel Curig. Buses from Porthmadog, Caernarfon and Betws-y-coed.
Facilities:	Shops and cafes in Beddgelert. Public toilets on the walk. Children's playground near the school.
Maps:	Ordnance Survey Explorer OL17; Landranger 115.

Beddgelert is an attractive, small village nestling below mountains beside the confluence of the rivers Afon Glaslyn and Afon Colwyn. The name, meaning Gelert's Grave, probably refers to St Kelert, an Irish missionary but, according to a much loved legend, it is associated with the grave of a hound. David Prichard, manager of the Royal Goat Hotel in the early 19th century, claimed to have found the grave and since then many visitors have

Walk 10
Beddgelert

North

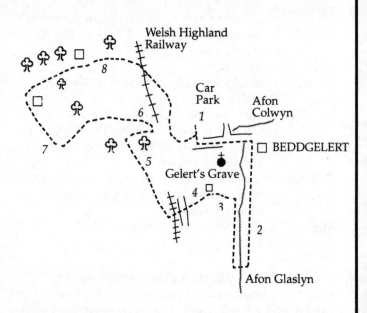

Welsh Highland Railway

Car Park

Afon Colwyn

□ BEDDGELERT

Gelert's Grave

Afon Glaslyn

52

visited Beddgelert to see where the faithful hound has been buried. Gelert belonged to Llywelyn Fawr who used to hunt around Beddgelert. One day when he returned from hunting, he was met by Gelert who was covered in blood. Entering the hunting lodge, he saw that his son`s cradle was overturned and he immediately assumed that Gelert had killed the baby. He plunged his sword into the hound then, too late, heard his son cry. Under the cot`s bedding, he found his son next to the body of a dead wolf. Gelert had killed the wolf to save his master`s son. Llywelyn, heartbroken, buried the hound and marked the grave with a large stone.

Walk directions:

1. From the car park, walk out to the road and turn left. When the road bends left over the bridge, leave it to take a road beside the river. It passes a café, gift shops and the public toilets. Cross a footbridge over Afon Glaslyn near the confluence with Afon Colwyn. Bear right to have the river on your right. Pass cottage gardens and go through a small gate. Follow the surfaced path and pass through another gate.

2. The path arrives at a footbridge next to the Welsh Highland Railway bridge. Cross the footbridge and follow the path as it swings to the right. Go through an unusually shaped gate and cross a small level bridge over a stream. Continue to the next gate.

3. Turn left on a path away from the river. When the path bends to the right, you will see a small gate on your left. The longer route goes through it but you may first wish to visit Gelert`s Grave which is under a tree a little further along the path. (If you are taking the short walk, after

visiting the grave, continue on the path and go through a gate then right to the river. Turn left beside it to the bridge used earlier then retrace your steps.)

4. For the longer route, go through the small gate and follow the path ahead to join a track. Maintain your direction to gates at the road. Cross with care to go up to the Welsh Highland Railway line and, taking care, cross it to a grassy path. After a few paces leave it by going right through a small gate. Follow a clear, fairly level path along the hillside. It crosses stepping stones over a stream and reaches a small gate. Go through it and, after a few paces, go left along the cemetery drive.

5. After about 30 metres, leave it to go right on a clear path through trees to a kissing-gate. Follow the left-hand fence to a corner then bear right over a small level footbridge. Walk along the path for about 70 metres then cross a footbridge on your right. Continue beside a left-hand wall to a broad gate in the wall. Pass through it and go ahead on a clear path and through a gap. Cross some stones and walk beside a right-hand fence and cross a little culvert. You will soon reach a footbridge over the Welsh Highland Railway.

6. Do not cross unless you wish to finish the walk here. Instead, turn left and follow the line of overhead wires to a gap in a wall. Continue along the clear path and you will soon have a wall on your right. Continue beside the wall to the end of the field and go through the gate (or climb the stile) in the corner. Walk ahead, veering slightly right away from the wall then, after a few paces, go left uphill to a gap in the top wall. Head towards a fence corner and keep on uphill, passing a small enclosure with trees on your right. Keep on uphill to arrive on a track

with superb views of Moel Hebog, and backwards views of the valley and Snowdon range.

7. Turn right along the track. Pass an old barn and, lower down, cross a flat bridge near houses. Follow the track around to the right and go downhill through tall pines and cross a line of the Welsh Highland Railway. Pass a house on the left, cross another line and ignore a level bridge on the right. After about 80 metres, at the end of farm buildings on the left, bear right over a level bridge and go through a gate.

8. Bear slightly left to follow a path alongside trees. Go right at a corner and soon leave the path to go left under a railway bridge. When the path divides, go right then left uphill. At steps on the left, walk ahead downhill and through a gate. Keep ahead to an access road then turn left to the main road, where you turn left to the start.

Beddgelert Forest

Route: This walk follows forest tracks, some of them uphill, to a lovely lake in a woodland setting.

Start: Beddgelert Forest car park.

Access: The car park is off the A4085, north of Beddgelert. Take a lane on the left half a mile north of the forest camp site, then go right on a track to the car park.

Facilities: Picnic tables at Llyn Llywelyn. Cafes in Beddgelert.

Maps: Ordnance Survey Explorer OL17; Landranger 115.

Beddgelert Forest is a magnificent, coniferous woodland on the eastern slopes of mountains in the Moel Hebog range. The trees were first planted in 1926 and many have been felled, opening up views of Snowdonia`s mountains. This walk takes you to a beautiful, small lake surrounded by trees below Moel Lefn. According to legend, the hollow holding the lake was made by a giant who jumped from a rock whilst taking part in a jumping contest with anther giant. It is a fine spot for a picnic.

Walk directions:
1. From the car park, take the lower track towards the entrance and, after a few paces, go right on a path. It goes downhill beside overhead wires and emerges on a track.

Walk 11
Beddgelert Forest

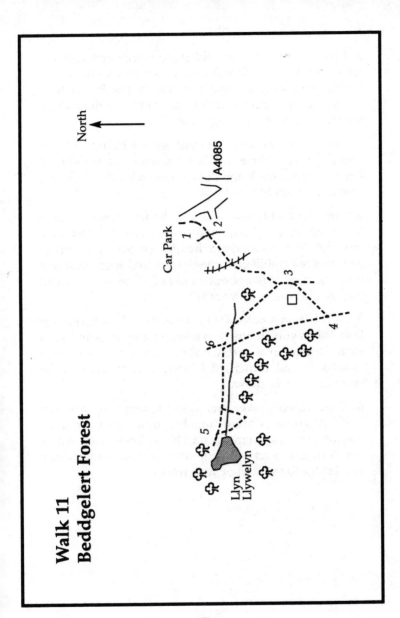

2. Turn right to cross an old stone bridge and ignore a track on the left. Follow the track as it crosses the Welsh Highland Railway line and curves to the left. Pass a drive to a house and ignore a track on the right. Continue along the main track beside a right-hand wall.

3. At the next track on the right, signed Hafod Ruffydd Uchaf, go right along it. When the track bends right, go left on a lesser track and pass around a barrier. Follow it uphill to a broad forest track.

4. Turn right and there will soon be fine views towards Snowdon. Ignore a path and track on the left and walk downhill to cross a bridge. Reach a crossroads of tracks and turn left uphill on a rough track and keep head at a track junction. After about another 200 metres, you will see Llyn Llywelyn on your left.

5. Turn left on a path. There are picnic tables beside the lake. When you are ready to leave, follow the path over a small bridge to a forest track. Turn left to the track crossroads and turn right to retrace your steps to the crossroads lower down.

6. Cross directly over and walk downhill on a rough track. A stream is heard tumbling down on your right. Stay on the track to emerge on a broad forest track, where you turn left to retrace your steps over the railway line and bridge to the start of your walk.

Dolwyddelan

Route: This short, interesting walk follows a forest track into the beautiful valley of Cwm Penamnen then returns along a Roman road, passing medieval ruins.

Start: Car park beside Dolwyddelan railway station.

Access: Leave the A5 for the A470 south of Betws-y-coed. At Dolwyddelan, take the road signposted to the railway station. Trains from Blaenau Ffestiniog, Llandudno and Llandudno Junction to Dolwyddelan (request stop). Buses from Blaenau Ffestiniog, Llandudno and Llandudno Junction to Dolwyddelan.

Facilities: Picnic tables at start and on the route. Shop, cafes and pub near the crossroads in Dolwyddelan. Public toilets near the crossroads.

Maps: Ordnance Survey OL18; Landranger 115.

Cwm Penamnen is a beautiful, forested valley with cliffs and a tumultuous river. The lane through the cwm follows the route of a Roman road, Sarn Elen, that linked the forts between Canovium at Caerhun near Conwy with Moridunum at Caernarfon. The ruins of Tai Penamnen are being excavated and there is an information board about the site.

The house once belonged to Maredudd ap Ieuan who was a tenant of Dolwyddelan Castle. He built the present

Walk 12
Dolwyddelan

North

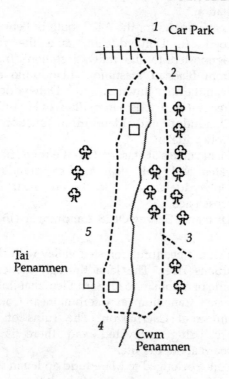

DOLWYDDELAN

church in the village about AD 1500 and gave the tenancy of his cottages in the Lledr Valley to men with skills in archery. There was a gang of notorious bandits at Ysbyty Ifan over the hills to the south who terrorised the district. His force of over one hundred men brought about some degree of law and order.

Walk directions:

1. From the car park walk out to the lane and turn left to cross the railway bridge. Bear left, ignore a terrace on the right and soon turn right along a track.

2. Pass a house on the left and walk around a gate across the track. Follow the rough track into the forest. If you look back you will have views of Moel Siabod and Dolwyddelan Castle on its rock. Continue along the track, steadily uphill.

3. On reaching a track on the right with a white footprint sign, go right along it. You will soon have open views. The track goes downhill then levels out. Turn right at a signpost for Pont Carreg Alltrem and cross a wooden footbridge over Afon Cwmpenamnen.

4. Follow the path up to the lane where there are picnic tables and great views towards the head of the valley. Turn right along the lane and pass the remains of Tai Penamnen on both sides of the lane. Further on, go through a gate across the lane.

5. After a few metres, you can see a waterfall below on your right and, in places, the lane passes close to the river. Go through another gate across the lane and walk downhill past houses. Follow the road to the right and cross the bridge over the railway lane to retrace your steps to the start.

Llyn Mair

Route:	After walking beside the lovely lake Llyn Mair, the route crosses the Ffestiniog Railway and follows a path to a viewpoint of the Ffestiniog Valley before returning beside another woodland lake.
Start:	Car park beside Llyn Mair.
Access:	East of Penrhyndeudraeth, leave the A487 at the Oakeley Arms for the B4410. A small car park is opposite the picnic area at Llyn Mair. You can also take the Ffestiniog Railway to Tan y Bwlch station, which is on the route.
Facilities:	Picnic tables on the walk. Café and toilets at Tan y Bwlch station on the Ffestiniog Railway, passed on the walk.
Maps:	Ordnance Survey Explorer 18; Landranger 124.

Llyn Mair is a pretty, woodland lake lying beside the road below Tan y Bwlch station on the Ffestiniog Railway. At the start of the walk is a picnic area beside the lake. You are likely to see ducks and woodland birds such as jays. In the summer months butterflies and dragonflies may be seen near the paths. Bluebells grow in some areas of the woods and water lilies may be seen on the lakes in the summer. Between Tan y Bwlch station and Llyn Mair, the walk follows part of a nature trail through the ancient woodlands.

The walk passes above the mansion Plas Tan y Bwlch which was for many years the home of the Oakeley

Walk 13
Llyn Mair

North

Ffestiniog Railway

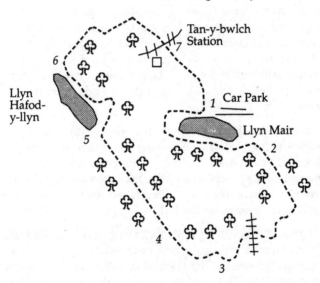

Tan-y-bwlch
Station

7

6

Llyn
Hafod-
y-llyn

5

1 Car Park

Llyn Mair

2

4

3

family who owned slate quarries at Blaenau Ffestiniog. They made many improvements to the estate and the village of Maentwrog across the valley. Llyn Mair and the lower mill pond provided water for water powered saw and flour mills in the Ffestiniog Valley. The Ffestiniog Railway station at Tan y Bwlch brought in supplies for the estate and took out timber. Plas Tan y Bwlch is now a study centre for the Snowdonia National Park.

Walk directions:

1. From the car park, cross the road and go through a gate to the picnic area beside Llyn Mair. Bear right along a track and go left on a path at a post marked 26. It crosses a stream and goes through a gap in a wall and then turns left. Cross a level footbridge below a pool and continue on the path beside the lake. After it joins a track at a gate, walk on beside the lake and, after it ends, join another track.

2. Bear right along the track. It goes slightly uphill and passes a pool on the left. After the track starts to go downhill and passes the end of the pool, take a path on the right. At a junction of paths, take the right-hand path. Ignore a path on the left at a bend, and walk uphill on the path as it zig-zags up the hill.

3. Cross the Ffestiniog Railway at Plas Tan y Bwlch Halt. Go through a little gate and bear left. There are views through the trees of the Ffestiniog Valley and the village of Maentwrog. The path passes above the mansion of Plas Tan Y Bwlch and winds through some magnificent beech trees before rising to a rocky viewpoint (take care). Continue along the path and go downhill a little to a path junction. Turn right and go through a gap in a wall to

continue on a path through woodlands. It crosses a little stream and passes coniferous trees then reaches a broad track. Turn left to another track junction.

4. Turn right and ignore another track on the right. Continuing ahead, you can see the FFestniog Railway line below on the right. Ignore a path on the left and a track on the right and, after another 40 metres, at a left bend, go right on a path to the lake Llyn Hafod y Llyn where there are picnic tables.

5. Follow the path beside the lake and continue along it as it bears left. The path soon veers right away from the lake, then swings left to rise to picnic tables above the lake. Continue along the path, looking out for water lilies on the lake, and emerge on a track.

6. Turn right along the track and go through a kissing-gate at a barrier. Turn right along the road and, after a few metres, go left on a lane. Walk uphill for about 200 metres then cross a stile on the right. Follow the path between a wall and fence to a footbridge over the Ffestiniog Railway at Tan y Bwlch station.

7. After crossing the footbridge, the route goes left beside the railway to where a lane joins from the right. Veer right to the gate for the nature trail and follow the path downhill to a footbridge over a stream near the car park at the start of the walk.

Coed y Brenin – Waterfalls

Route: This walk follows a fairly level forest track
                past two waterfalls and ruins of a gold mine.
                It then returns on the opposite side of Afon
                Mawddach and crosses a footbridge to the
                start.

Start: Tyddyn Gwladys car park.

Access: Leave the A470 for a lane on the northern
                side of the village of Ganllwyd, five miles
                north of Dolgellau. Follow the lane for about
                one and a half miles to Tyddyn Gwladys car
                park.

Facilities: Picnic tables at the car park. Public toilets in
                Ganllwyd car park. Café and children's
                playground at Coed y Brenin Visitor Centre
                (not on the route).

Maps: Ordnance Survey Explorer OL18;
                Landranger 124.

The highlights of this walk are the waterfalls of Pistyll y
Cain and Rhaeadr Mawddach, best seen after heavy rain.
You will also pass ruins of Gwynfynydd gold mine. This
was originally a lead mine and after gold was discovered
here in 1864, it became one of the most important gold
mines in Meirionnydd. More than two hundred men
worked at the mine, living in barracks. The mine
amalgamated with the Clogau mine in 1900 but
Gwynfynydd closed in 1916, although it has been worked
for short periods since then. A waterwheel below
Rhaeadr Mawddach provided power for the mill. Rings

Walk 14
Coed y Brenin

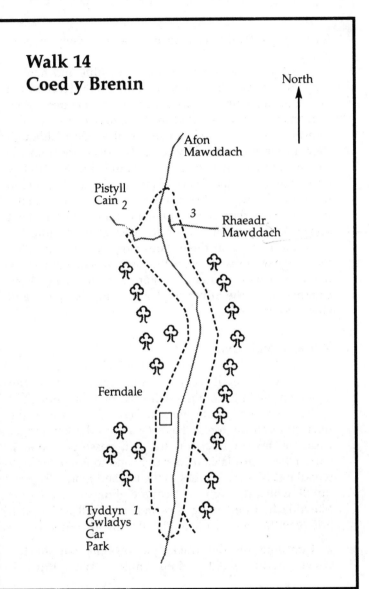

North

Afon
Mawddach

Pistyll
Cain 2

3

Rhaeadr
Mawddach

Ferndale

Tyddyn 1
Gwladys
Car
Park

for the royal family have been made from Gwynfynydd gold.

Coed y Brenin is known for its wildlife and herons, dippers and wagtails may be seen around the river. Listen and look for jays and woodpeckers in the trees. Pied flycatchers may be spotted in the summer months. The forest is also the home of a herd of fallow deer, although they are only occasionally seen. The deer are from the former Nannau estate which was founded in AD 1100 by Cadwgan, son of the Prince of Powys. The land stayed in the same family for hundreds of years, but eventually passed by marriage to the Vaughan family. After the First World War, part of the estate was sold for forestry. Covering more than three thousand acres, it was called the Vaughan Forest. In 1935, the forest was given the new name of Coed y Brenin – Forest of the King – to commemorate the Silver Jubilee of King George V and Queen Mary.

Walk directions:

1. From the car park, go out to the lane and turn right. After a few metres, it becomes a track. Ignore a track with a gate on the left. Continue with the river on your right and go through a gate marked Ferndale to follow the track through the forest. Pass houses on the left and, at Ferndale, take a track on the left, passing around a barrier. Pass Ferndale on your right and continue through woodland. The track bears to the left and gradually goes uphill, whilst through the trees are glimpses of Rhaeadr Mawddach. After going downhill you will arrive at a bridge with a good view of Pistyll Cain on your left.

2. Continue on the track, passing the site of the Gwynfynydd Gold Mine mill. Pass through

rhododendrons and cross an old bridge on the right spanning the river. The track veers to the right uphill to another track.

3. Turn right and walk downhill, passing a bench. Continuing along the track, you will see Ferndale on the opposite side of Afon Mawddach. Ignore a track on the left and, further on, at a curve in the track, take a path to the aerial footbridge over the river. Follow a footpath that gradually rises, with the river on your right, to Tyddyn Gwladys car park.

Harlech – Castle and Beach

Route: The walk visits a stunning viewpoint of Harlech castle and Cardigan Bay before descending to a path winding through the sand dunes to the beach.

Start: Harlech Castle.

Access: Harlech can be reached from the A496 and is on the Machynlleth – Pwllheli Cambrian coast railway line. Buses from Barmouth, Blaenau Ffestiniog and the Oakley Arms at Maentwrog. Car parks signposted.

Facilities: Shops, cafes and pubs in the town. Public toilets near the start and passed on the walk. Children`s playground near the castle and on the walk.

Maps: Ordnance Survey Explorer OL18; Landranger 124.

Harlech Castle is one of a chain built by Edward 1 in the 13th century to suppress the Welsh. Designed by Master James of St George, who became constable, it took only seven years to build. At that time the castle had access to the sea and provisions for the garrison were brought in by ship. However, it was taken by Owain Glyndwr in 1404 and he held it for four years. Harlech Castle was the last Lancastrian stronghold to fall during the Wars of the Roses and it was this resistance that inspired the song `Men of Harlech`. Again, during the Civil War, it was the last castle to be taken by the Parliamentarians.

    Near the castle is a sculpture of `The Two Kings` by

Walk 15
Harlech Castle and Beach

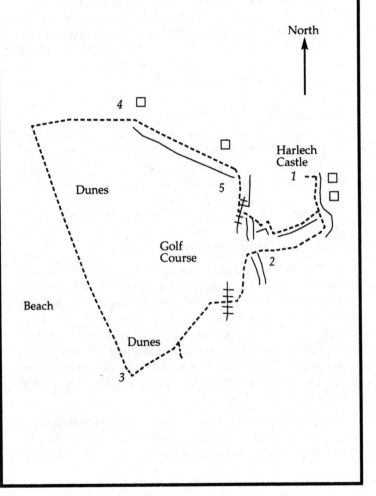

North

4

Harlech
Castle

1

Dunes

5

Golf
Course

2

Beach

Dunes

3

Ivor Roberts Jones. It represents a story from the Mabinogi where Bran is carrying the body of his nephew Gwern, son of Branwen, who was killed during a war with the Irish.

The walk takes you to a fine viewpoint of the castle with the northern mountains of Snowdonia in the distance. Further on in the walk, you pass Coleg Harlech, an adult education college that opened in 1927. From the path through the dunes you will have more views of the castle. Look out for wild flowers.

Walk directions:

1. From the castle, go uphill to the main street and turn right. Pass some shops, the church and a car park. Continue along the main road and, at a left bend, where the pavement ends, go right on a path with a footpath sign. To your right is a fine viewpoint of Harlech Castle, Cardigan Bay and northern Snowdonia`s mountains. Return to the path and walk downhill. Follow the wall on the left to a road almost opposite the theatre.

2. Cross the road and go through a gap in a fence on the opposite side. Go down a few steps then bear right between walls to more steps. Emerge on a lane and turn left. After about 250 metres, bear right through a small gate to go over a level crossing. After another gate, go left on a wide path to where it makes a sharp left bend. Here, leave it go ahead on a clear path that heads towards sand dunes. Go through the dunes and up and down a sandhill to the beach.

3. Bear right along the beach for almost a mile then leave it at Harlech`s main entrance to the beach. It is marked by a tall post with red and white bands. The wide path

passes between posts which are frequently buried by sand. Further along it is surfaced and passes through the golf course until it reaches gates. On your left is a car park and public toilets.

4. Follow the road ahead in the direction of Harlech Castle. Opposite the entrance to the secondary school is a small children's playground in a playing field. Continuing along the road, you will pass a shop on your right and emerge at the main road.

5. Turn right and, after a few paces, bear right through a small gate and follow a path parallel to the road. Ignore a footbridge on the right and go left on a path to a gate. Cross the railway line with care to another gate and go over the main road to a road going uphill in the direction of the town centre. Follow the steep road to the second left bend, then go ahead along a narrower road. It bends to the left and, at a corner, passes a very narrow house. Here go left up steps to Harlech's main street. Go left to the start at the castle or, after a few paces, bear right on a path to the long stay car park.

Harlech – Views from Above

Route: This walk climbs the hillside above Harlech and follows paths offering superb views of Cardigan Bay and Snowdonia's mountains.

Start: Long stay car park in Harlech.

Access: Harlech town centre is on the B4573, off the A496. Buses from Barmouth, Blaenau Ffestniog and the Oakeley Arms at Maentwrog. Car parks signposted.

Facilities: Shops, cafes and pubs in the town. Public toilets near the castle and the short stay car park. Children's playground near the castle.

Maps: Ordnance Survey Explorer OL18; Landranger 124.

On a clear day, from the hill slopes above Harlech you will have superb views of beaches and estuaries, Cardigan Bay and the Llŷn peninsula and also some of the mountains of northern Snowdonia.. From the top lane you can see the Rhinog range.

This area of Snowdonia has many prehistoric sites and shortly after the walk leaves the top lane, you pass near the foundations of two ancient settlements known as Muriau Gwyddelod (*'Irishmen's walls'*). The hut groups were enclosed by stone walls which are still well preserved.

Walk directions:

1. At the long stay car park, have your back to the road

Walk 16
Harlech Views from Above

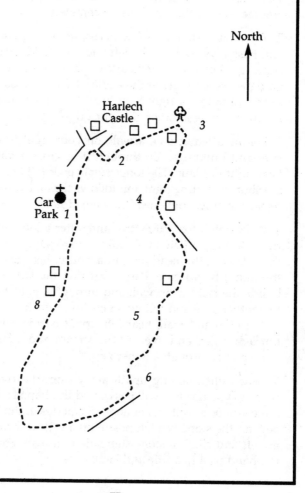

North

Harlech
Castle

Car
Park *1*

2

3

4

5

6

7

8

and, from the right side of the car park, take a path downhill through the park. Cross a footbridge and follow the path to the main road in Harlech. Turn right to a crossroads and then turn right, passing the Lion Hotel. Walk uphill and soon go left on a narrow road that emerges on another road near a cemetery.

2. Turn left and, after a few paces, ignore a path on the left. Pass Llys Bach on the left and, at a field gate on the right, go left on a waymarked path. It passes above gardens and emerges at the end of a drive. Cross directly over and follow a right-hand wall through a small gate. Before reaching another gate, turn right uphill.

3. Follow a fence, then a wall, on your right to a broad gate and buildings. Go through it to cross a yard then bear right to a lane. The longer walk goes left here, whilst the short one turns right and follows the lane downhill to rejoin the outer route near the Lion Hotel.

4. Walk uphill for 350 metres and, after a left bend, turn right through a gate at a walking man signpost. Follow the grassy path ahead and, at a house, bear left and go through a broad gate. Pass a barn on the left and walk beside the right-hand wall and through a gate. Slant left to another gate and follow an enclosed track. At the end of the left-hand wall, bear left uphill beside a wall. Go through a gap and over a little stream and, after a few more paces, through another gap.

5. Bear right, slanting uphill away from the right-hand wall. As you rise you will pass an oddly shaped stone and there will be a wall corner about 50 metres to the left. Just beyond the stone is a tall post with a yellow arrow. Here go left and climb a stone step stile in a wall. Follow the left-hand wall to a stile and lane.

6. Turn right along the lane. After about 300 metres, climb a ladder stile on the right. Walk ahead a few metres (to your right is the ancient settlement Muriau Gwyddelod), then slant left, at first through gorse, to the far corner where there is a stone step stile in the wall. Cross it and follow the left-hand wall to the field corner then go left through a gap.

7. Immediately turn right then swing right again to follow an enclosed track towards the sea. On reaching a gap in the right-hand wall, go through it and bear left to follow the wall through another gap. Now slant right on a visible path to a waymarked stone stile in a wall. Slant to the right, away from the right-hand wall, and pass above a hollow. Have overhead wires to your left and go through a gap in a wall. Walk downhill, passing under the wires. Go through a gap near a wall corner and head diagonally downhill to a broad gate.

8. Follow an enclosed path that veers to the right and passes behind a house. It goes left to the road. Walk along the pavement beside a right-hand wall to the corner then bear right for a few paces to another road. Go right and soon go left on a track, passing a house on the left. Follow the track between walls, passing a caravan site. On reaching a road, turn right for 20 metres. When the road bends left, leave it to go ahead past barrier posts onto another road. Follow it to a junction then go right to the car park.

Llanbedr – Aberartro Woodlands

Route:	This is a delightful walk through mature woodlands to pasture offering open views towards the Rhinog mountain range. The return passes Capel Salem, known for its famous painting.
Start:	Bridge over Afon Artro in the centre of Llanbedr.
Access:	Llanbedr is on the A496, south of Harlech. Car park near the railway station and on street parking in the minor road past the Victoria Inn. Llanbedr is on the Machynlleth -Pwllheli Cambrian Coast railway line. Buses from Barmouth, Blaenau Ffestiniog and the Oakeley Arms at Maentwrog.
Facilities:	Shops, pubs and restaurant in Llanbedr. Public toilets a few metres along the minor road past the Victoria Inn. Children`s playground at the beginning and end of the walk.
Maps:	Ordnance Survey Explorer OL18; Landranger 124.

Coed Aberartro is a mature woodland of beech, sessile oak, birch and other deciduous trees. In the spring you may spot flowers such as wood sorrel, wood avens and dog mercury. The path goes above an impressive gorge and crosses Afon Cwmnantcol to lanes and fields with beautiful views of the surrounding countryside.

The walk passes Capel Salem where you can see

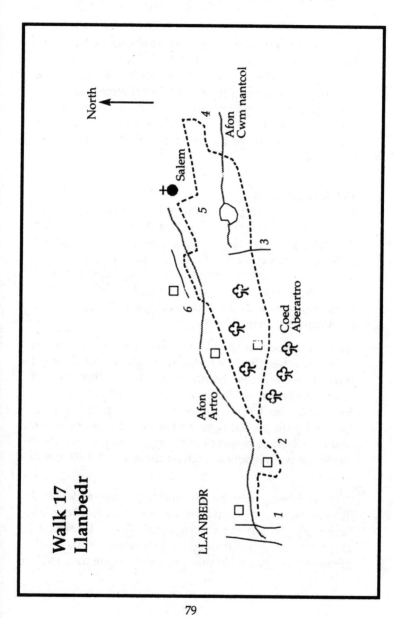

Walk 17
Llanbedr

North

LLANBEDR

Afon Artro

Salem

Afon Cwm nantcol

Coed Aberartro

1 2 3 4 5 6

copies of the famous painting made by Curnow Vosper in 1908 of the chapel`s congregation. The painting was shown at the Royal Watercolours Society Exhibition in London and was bought by Lord Leverhulme. Since then the original painting has hung in Port Sunlight art gallery. Before the chapel was built in the mid 19th century, baptisms were carried out in a pool of Afon Artro below the chapel.

Walk directions:

1. From the opposite of the bridge to the Victoria Inn, take a footpath down steps to have Afon Artro on your left. Go through a kissing-gate and with trees on your left, pass a children`s playground and walk through a field to a kissing-gate. Turn right and soon go through a gate to have a wall on your left. At buildings, bear left through a broad gate and walk through a farmyard, then follow the farm drive to a lane.

2. Turn left and you will soon have the river below on your left. When the lane forks, veer right and walk uphill through woodlands. Ignore footpaths on the left and right. At a house, the lane curves to the right and left to a fork. Take the left-hand track and go through a gate. Ignore a path on the right and walk through along the main track. After it curves to the right and passes a short section of wall, ignore a track on the left and walk uphill to a lane.

3. Cross directly over the lane and follow the track ahead. Take extreme care if you leave the route to descend to the bridge on the left for a view of the gorge. Continuing along the track, go through a gate across it and walk above the reservoir. Go through another gate then left at

a fork to cross a footbridge over Afon Cwmnantcol . Walk ahead to an access track and cross over it then go uphill to reach a lane.

4. Turn right and go through a gate next to a cattle grid. After about 100 metres, go left on a path enclosed by walls to a small gate. Follow the left-hand wall downhill and around a left-hand corner. At the next corner, climb steps in a wall then continue beside a left-hand wall. Bear right before a gate, then left, gradually going downhill beside the wall to a gate. Walk through the middle of the field to a wall then bear right beside it. When the wall goes left, maintain your direction beside trees, to reach a small gate.

5. Turn right along the lane and, after a few metres, you will see Capel Salem on your right. The lane enters woodlands and descends to a cattle grid and another lane. Turn right over the bridge then left on another road. Follow it for 250 metres to Pentre Gwynfryn and, after another 80 metres, go left down steps to cross a footbridge over Afon Arto.

6. Bear right on a path beside the river. It becomes a track and passes a farmhouse. Ignore paths off it and follow the track to the fork in the lane walked earlier, then retrace your steps to the start of the walk.

Dyffryn Ardudwy

Route:	Field and woodland paths with several stiles of different types. On the return, the walk passes the Dyffryn Ardudwy Neolithic burial chamber.
Start:	Car park in Station Road near the crossroads and shops in Dyffryn Ardudwy. Bus stops nearby.
Access:	Dyffryn Ardudwy is on the A496 between Barmouth and Harlech. Buses from Barmouth, the Oakeley Arms at Maentwrog and Blaenau Ffestiniog. Dyffryn Ardudwy is on the Machynlleth-Pwllheli Cambrian Coast railway line. The station is about half a mile from the start of the walk.
Facilities:	Shops and children's playground near the start and end of the walk.
Maps:	Ordnance Survey Explorer OL18; Landranger 124.

This fairly easy walk explores the attractive, varied countryside around Dyffryn Ardudwy. After a short, uphill stretch on a path and lane, the route passes through woods as well as fields offering extensive coastal views. Look out for spring and summer flowers.

The Neolithic burial chamber, passed near the end of the walk, consists of two chambers dating from about the 4th millennium BC. The lower, smaller chamber is the older and both have a capstone. Excavation in 1960 revealed ceremonial offerings of broken pottery near both

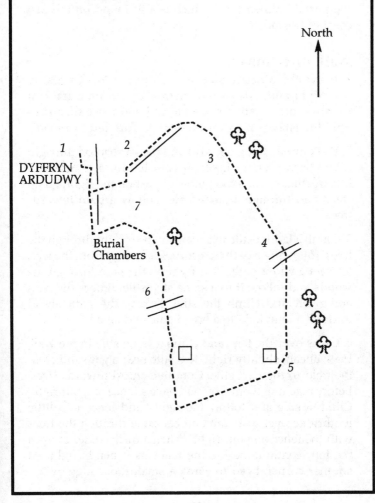

Walk 18
Dyffryn Ardudwy

North

1

DYFFRYN
ARDUDWY

2

3

7

Burial
Chambers

4

6

5

chambers and in the larger tomb were Bronze Age cremated bones. The older chamber had its own cairn and, after the erection of the larger tomb, a huge cairn was built to enclose the two tombs. The burial site is of the portal dolmen type, which is also found on the east coast of Ireland.

Walk directions:

1. Leave the car park and turn left to the A496. Cross it, bear right and, after a few metres, go left on a track. It narrows into a path between a wall and fence then goes uphill to emerge on a surfaced track. Turn left to a road.

2. Walk uphill along the road and pass a road on the right called Bryn Awelon. Look on your left for a cemetery. A little further on, at a footpath signpost on the right, go up steps and through a small gate. Follow a path towards trees.

3. Climb a ladder stile in a wall and bear right through the trees, following a path that curves left away from the wall to meet a wider path. Bear right on the path through the woods and follow it to a stone step stile. Ignore the path going left and climb the stile. Follow the path ahead through a long field to a broad gate and lane.

4. Cross over the lane and climb a stone stile in the wall. Walk ahead, slightly right, to a stile near a gate and cross the field to the next stile. Continue ahead towards trees. Before reaching them, you will have a fence on your right. Climb a stile and follow the right-hand fence to a little footbridge over a stream and continue through the trees with the fence on your right. When a track comes in from the left, continue beside the fence as it bends right. At another corner, head towards a small footbridge over a

stream and follow the path to a small gate and emerge on a lane.

5. Follow the lane downhill towards the sea. Further down, go through a gate across the lane and pass below overhead wires. Before reaching houses, climb a stone stile on the right. It has a little gate on the top. Veer right to a small gate on the left and cross a wide wall. Continue to steps and a small gate. On the other side of this wall, go right beside the wall and through a gate. There are farm buildings across to your right. Slant right up the field to join a track. Bear left, passing buildings on your right and go through a gate across the track.

6. Emerge on a lane and cross directly over the lane and through a gate into a field. Slant right uphill to a wall then continue with the wall on your right. Cross a broken wall and climb a stone stile in a corner. Cross a stream and follow a path downhill through trees to a gate in the left corner. Go ahead, slanting left through a field to a small gate.

7. On your left are the Dyffryn Ardudwy burial chambers. Lower down the path, a kissing-gate gives access. After visiting the site, continue on the path to a small gate and the A496 road. Turn right along the pavement to the start.

Talybont

Route: Woodland and riverside paths and a quiet lane passing a Neolithic burial chamber.

Start: Talybont car park off the A496 and near the bridge over Afon Ysgethin.

Access: Talybont is on the A496, north of Barmouth. Buses from Barmouth, Blaenau Ffestiniog and the Oakeley Arms at Maentwrog. Bus stop near the car park.

Facilities: Shop nearby. Public toilets near the car park. Ysgethin Inn on the route.

Maps: Ordnance Survey Explorer OL18; Landranger 124.

This fine walk follows the tumbling Afon Ysgethin through the attractive Cors y Gedol broad leaved woodlands. Bluebells, wood sorrel and other woodland flowers can be seen here in spring. For several centuries, Cors y Gedol was the home of the Vaughan family who involved themselves in local government. On the route you pass the Ysgethin Inn, a former woollen mill. After leaving the river, the walk emerges near Llety Lloegr, which was once a lodging and shoeing station for drovers taking Welsh cattle on the long journey to markets in England.

Further along the route, the Neolithic burial chamber, locally known as Arthur`s Quoit, stands on the left side of the lane. It is said that King Arthur threw the large capstone from the top of the hill called Moelfre and the indentations on the stone were made by his fingers. Some

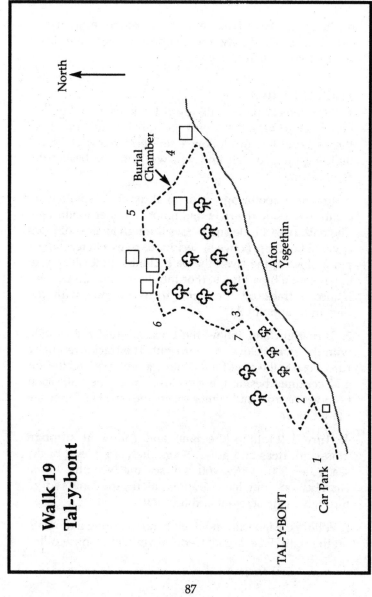

Walk 19
Tal-y-bont

North

Burial Chamber

Afon Ysgethin

TAL-Y-BONT

Car Park

87

of the stones have fallen and the capstone rests on two side stones. Originally, the chamber would have been covered with earth and stones.

Walk directions:

1. From the car park, walk towards the river and go left on a track to have the Afon Ysgethin on your right. Pass the Ysgethin Inn and follow a path beside a wall. Pass a building on your left and you will soon be beside the river again.

2. Ignore a footbridge and go through a small gate. Continue beside the river and ignore another footbridge. The path rises a little and passes through an area of moss covered boulders between deciduous trees. On reaching a point close to the river, the path climbs quite steeply to emerge on a broad track. (For the short walk, go left and ignore a track on the right, then continue with the directions at point 7.)

3. Turn right and follow the track gradually downhill, with the river below on your right. The track eventually runs close to the river for a while. Ignore a path on the left and continue beside the river to a gate. The path soon becomes narrow and climbs to emerge on a lane opposite Llety Lloegr.

4. Turn left along the lane and follow it through grassland, trees and gorse. Soon, there are views of the sea. After 300 metres you will see the Neolithic burial chamber on your left. Continue along the lane and go through a gate across it and turn left.

5. Follow the lane around a left bend, ignoring a footpath on the right. Pass Cors y Gedol Farm and a house called

Llysfaen on your right. Further along, where a drive leaves it for Cors y Gedol Hall, the lane bends left between tall trees. After 200 metres, go left through a gate.

6. Walk along the broad, walled track and go through a gate across it. Ignore the immediate path on your right but, after a few more metres, you will reach a fork. Here, go right to have a stream on your right for a short distance. You will reach a junction of paths near a right-hand fence. Bear left, ignoring paths off. Follow a broad track between overgrown walls. On reaching another track, turn right. This is the point where you join the short walk.

7. Follow the track downhill, with Afon Ysgethin below on your left. Cross a level footbridge over a stream and go through a gate across the track. Join an access lane and pass bungalows on your right. Emerge on a road, but leave it immediately by going left through a gate to pass a house on your right. Have a fence on your right and rejoin the path beside the river. Turn right to retrace your steps to the start.

Barmouth

Route:	A gradual climb on paths and tracks offering stunning views of Barmouth, the Afon Mawddach estuary and coastline.
Start:	The main car park opposite the beach.
Access:	Barmouth is on the A496. The resort is on The Machynlleth-Pwllheli Cambrian Coast railway line. Buses from Chester, Wrexham, Blaenau Ffestiniog and the Oakeley Arms at Maentwrog.
Facilties:	Shops, cafes, pubs and public toilets in Barmouth.
Maps:	Ordnance Survey Explorer OL18; Landranger 124.

Barmouth is a popular, small holiday resort lying at the mouth of the beautiful Afon Mawddach estuary. Early travellers were enraptured by the stunning scenery. During the late 18th and early 19th centuries, Barmouth was a busy port with many shipyards along the shores of the river. The coming of the railway and the opening of the viaduct in 1867 brought many more visitors to the little town, which had become known for its sands and sea bathing.

On much of the walk you can enjoy magnificent views of Barmouth, Afon Mawddach estuary and Cardigan Bay. The walk climbs the hillside to Dinas Oleu, the first property to be given to the National Trust. It was donated by Mrs Fanny Talbot who lived at Ty`n y Ffynnon nearby. Further on, you can visit the Frenchman`s Grave.

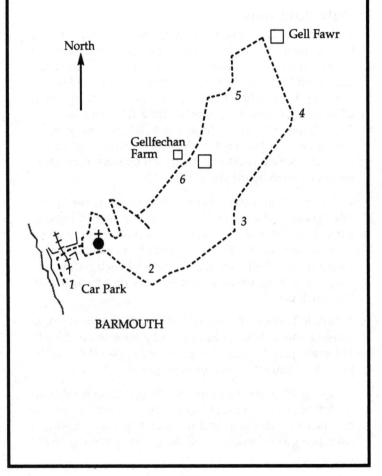

Walk 20
Barmouth

North

Gell Fawr

5

4

Gellfechan
Farm

6

3

2

1   Car Park

BARMOUTH

Auguste Guyard, who died in 1883, lived in a cottage that was one of several given by Mrs Talbot to the writer and social reformer John Ruskin. Ruskin was experimenting with social living and Guyard taught his neighbours about growing vegetables and herbs.

Walk directions:

1. From the car park, turn right and pass the Leisure Centre, then bear right. Cross the level crossing and go over a road to continue ahead to the main road. Turn right and soon bear left over the road at the pedestrian crossing. Turn right for a few paces then go left up Dinas Olau Road. Cross over another little road and walk up Tan y Craig. It bends right to a fork, where you go right. Take a path on the left which rises gradually up the hill and, on reaching another path, go left up steps then left to an information board about Dinas Oleu.

2. Bear right on a path that winds through gorse up the hill. Ignore paths on the left and go through a kissing-gate. Walk ahead with a wall on the right. Further along a small gate and a path leads to the Frenchman`s Grave. Continue beside the wall, then pass a bench on the left. After a few more paces, go left at a fork on a narrow path to a small gate.

3. Turn left on a path parallel to the wall. Follow the path when it bends right to have a rocky hillside on the left. The path goes through two gates and passes slabs on the left where you may see rock climbers.

4. Emerge on a lane and turn left along it. Ignore a stile on the left but climb a stile at a gate across the lane. Continue to a house, Gell Fawr, and immediately after passing in front of it go left beside a wall then a fence, passing an old

building on the right. Follow the fence to a small gate.

5. Go ahead over a tiny, level bridge and through reeds to another path. Turn right through a gate and walk above a little valley. On reaching a gap into a field, turn left to have a wall on your right and follow it to the ruins of Cellfechan Farm. Go slightly right downhill to the lowest building and pass it on your right.

6. Follow a track between walls and go through a gate across it. Lower down, a lesser track joins from the left. Here, bear right with the main track, which soon swings to the left. Look out on your right for gates, and go through the small gate onto a path which passes above the church. Continue to a lane then turn left down the steep hill. Turn right to pass houses then go left to the main road. Turn left to cross at traffic lights, then go left and right to the start.

Morfa Mawddach

Route: This lovely, short walk leads to Afon
              Mawddach estuary and returns through
              marshland, a nature reserve and along the
              trackbed of a former railway.

Start: Car park at Morfa Mawddach railway halt.

Access: South-west of Dolgellau, leave the A493 on a
              lane signposted for the railway halt at Morfa
              Mawddach. Morfa Mawddach is a request
              stop on the Machynlleth-Pwllheli Cambrian
              Coast railway line,

Facilities: Picnic tables and public toilets near the car
              park.

Maps: Ordnance Survey Explorer OL23:
              Landranger 124.

Afon Mawddach estuary is one of the most beautiful in
Europe. Look out for cormorants, herons, oystercatchers
and other waders. From the riverbank are great views of
the half-mile long railway viaduct across the estuary
which opened in 1867. For one hundred years a railway
ran between Morfa Mawddach and Dolgellau, from
where it continued to Ruabon, linking the Cambrian coast
with north-west England. Slate and copper were
exported. The line closed in 1965 because of lack of profits
and the former trackbed between Morfa Mawdach and
Dolgellau is now a walking and cycling trail. Some of the
surrounding land is now a nature reserve and the Arthog
Bog is a Site of Special Scientific interest. Reed buntings
and warblers may be spotted.

Walk 21
Morfa Mawddach

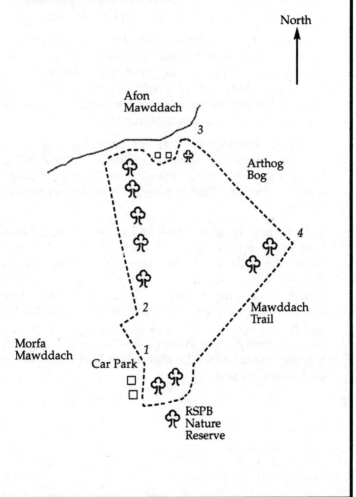

North

Afon Mawddach

Arthog Bog

3

Arthog Bog

4

Mawddach Trail

Morfa Mawddach

2

1

Car Park

RSPB Nature Reserve

Walk directions:

1. From the car park, walk back towards the lane and veer left at the toilets to follow the track that runs behind the car park. Continue with the railway line on your left and go through a gate on your right at a footpath signpost.

2. On reaching a rough track, turn left to have a rocky hill on your right. Walk towards the estuary and cross an embankment. Further on, veer right beside Afon Mawddach. At houses, bear right and follow the track as it bends left behind the gardens. On reaching a lane, go left towards the river and then turn right.

3. Before reaching the gate for Bryn Glyn, go right through a small gate. Ignore a path on the left and follow the raised path through marshland. Continue through gates and beside a field to emerge on the former railway line.

4. Turn right along the track and cross a bridge. Pass a long bench on the right and after another 100 metres, there is a path on the left into Cors Arthog Nature Reserve. Here you have the option of staying on the broad track and following it back to the start. Alternatively, turn left on the path to cross a footbridge and go through a kissing-gate. Bear right on a path to a junction, then go right to meet a lane. Turn right and, after passing houses, rejoin the Mawddach Trail and follow it back to the car park.

Fairbourne

Route:	This varied walk climbs into a valley in the hills above Friog, then returns beside the salt marshes of the Afon Mawddach estuary.
Start:	Car park in Station Road near Fairbourne railway station.
Access:	Fairbourne is a small resort off the A493, south-west of Dolgellau. It is on the Machynlleth-Pwllheli Cambrian Coast railway line. Buses from Dolgellau, Machynlleth and Aberystwyth. Can also be reached from Barmouth by ferry and miniature steam railway in the summer months.
Facilities:	Shop and café in Fairbourne. Public toilets near the car park at the start and at Morfa Mawddach. Picnic tables at Morfa Mawddach.
Maps:	Ordnance Survey Exploreer OL23; Landranger 124.

Fairbourne came into being in the late 19th century when the miller Arthur McDougall bought land on the coast near Friog to build the holiday resort. A tramway was built to carry the materials for the construction of the village and it became a steam railway in 1916.

The walk climbs into the hills behind Friog, passing near slate quarries which operated in the late 19th and early 20th centuries. The embankment beside Afon Mawddach salt marshes was built in the 19h century to

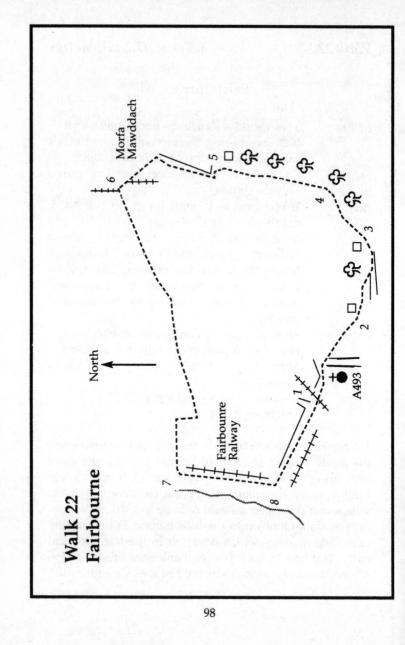

Walk 22
Fairbourne

North →

Morfa Mawddach

Fairbourne Ralway

A493

reclaim land for farming and building.

Walk directions:

1. From Station Road, turn left and cross the railway line at the level crossing. Continue along the road, passing the church on your right, to the A493. Turn right and soon go left along Ffordd y Ysgol. After about 60 metres, go right up steps at a footpath signpost and follow an enclosed path to steps. Go through a kissing-gate and beside a right-hand fence. The path veers left to a small gate and field. Follow the path towards houses.

2. Turn left past a house and go through a gate. Cross a track and walk ahead on a path, with a fence on the right, to a gate then follow a clear path downhill through trees to a gate and lane. Turn left uphill along the lane and follow it around to the left until it separates into two drives, then go right through a gate onto a track.

3. The track soon bends to the left, passing above a garden. Go through a kissing-gate and walk uphill with a fence on the left. At a fork, take the left-hand path beside a fence. At another fork, continue beside the fence and walk downhill, passing a quarry on the left.

4. Climb a ladder stile and continue beside a fence and wall, ignoring a path on the right. After another stile, veer left through gorse, then right at a fence to the next stile. Continue along an enclosed path to a stile and cross over a track. Have a wall on your right then go through a kissing-gate on the right and walk downhill. Go through trees to a ladder stile which is to the left of a field. Follow the right-hand fence to a drive and go left. When the drive bends right, go through a gate on the left to the A493.

5. Cross the road with care and turn left, then soon right along a road. Ignore a footpath on the right and pass houses on the left. Soon afterwards, join a track (Mawddach Trail) that runs parallel to the road. Pass picnic tables, public toilets and a car park at Morfa Mawddach. Soon go left through a small gate and cross the railway line to another gate.

6. Follow the enclosed path ahead and at a corner go left to a stile. Walk along the embankment with views across the estuary to Barmouth. Climb another stile and pass a rocky hill on the left. The path veers right between fences, over a channel, and around bends of the embankment to eventually emerge on a road.

7. Turn left at a halt of the Fairbourne Railway. It is possible to cross the railway line and walk between the line and the sea wall. Shortly after Golf Halt there is access to the beach. Further along there is a surfaced path beside the sea wall.

8. When the railway line bends away from the sea, bear left to follow the road to the car park at the start of the walk.

Walk 23 ᐤ S 2 or 4.5 miles/3.2 or 7.2 kilometres

Arthog Waterfalls and Llynnau Cregennen

Route: This beautiful walk climbs through woodlands, passing waterfalls, then visits one of the Cregennen lakes before returning along tracks and lanes.

Start: Car park near the Mawddach Trail at Arthog.

Access: Leave the A493 south-west of Arthog church for a lane at a corner building, signed Min-y-Don. Buses from Dolgellau, Machynlleth and Aberystwyth to Arthog.

Facilities: Picnic tables at car park at start. Toilets in car park at Llynnau Cregennen.

Maps: Ordnance Survey Explorer OL23; Landranger 124.

After climbing through woodlands, and passing waterfalls, the walk emerges at an old bridge over Afon Arthog, a good picnic spot. The short walk leaves the longer route here by following the lane downhill. Over the bridge, and to the right, are grass covered old stone banks that are the foundations of a medieval court called Llys Bradwen. Further into the longer walk, you can see the remains of a Bronze Age stone circle.

Llynnau Cregennen are two beautiful lakes that were given to the National Trust by Major Wynne-Jones in memory of his two sons who were killed during the Second World War.

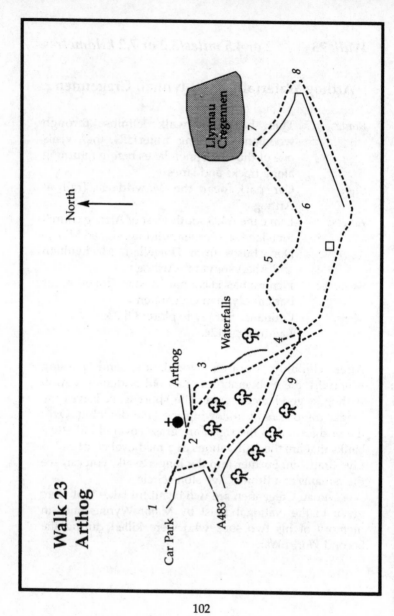

Walk 23
Arthog

North

Llynnau Cregennen

Waterfalls

Car Park

Arthog

A483

1 2 3 4 5 6 7 8 9

Walk directions:

1. At the car park, walk back through the entrance and turn right along the lane. Climb a stile on the left and follow an embankment beside Afon Arthog. It passes between gorse bushes to a stile. Continue with a fence on your left to the churchyard then go right beside the wall to a kissing-gate and the A493.

2. Cross the road with care and turn left for a few paces. When you are opposite the churchyard gate, go right up steps to a small gate and follow the path uphill. Take care as it passes above the river. Emerge on a track and turn left.

3. After following this track for about 40 metres, go right on a narrow path. Afon Arthog is tumbling down on your left. The path bends to the right at a point where there are views of a small waterfall on your left. Continue along the path and cross a ladder stile, then walk along the edge of woodlands with a field on your right. Higher up there are good views of more waterfalls. Continue along the rough, but obvious path, crossing stiles, until you emerge on a track. For the short walk, bear right to a stile and lane and skip all route directions to point 9.

4. For the longer walk, go ahead and cross an old bridge over the river. Walk uphill on a path to a track then turn left. On your left are great views of Afon Mawddach. Go through a gate across the track and ignore a track on the left. Pass through another gate into a field and bear right beside the wall.

5. Go through a gate and walk through another field. After the next gate, look to your right to see a small stone circle. Continue beside the right-hand wall to a wall corner at a footpath signpost. Bear left beside the wall. It

bends to the right and, after another gate, you reach another footpath signpost.

6. Turn left, uphill. The path veers slightly right away from the wall to avoid high ground. It then goes back towards the wall and follows it to a corner stile. Slant left over the hill then downhill to the road at Llynnau Cregennen. The walk goes right here, but the car park and toilets are along the lane to your left.

7. With the lake on your left, turn right along the lane. Go through a gate across it and look for a standing stone on your left. Pass through another gate across the lane and walk downhill to emerge on another lane.

8. Turn right and go through a gate across the lane. Ignore a track on the right and one on the left. After about another 120 metres, turn right on a grassy track towards a gate in a wall. Go through the gate and bear left beside the wall and through a gap. Bear right, pass a ruin on your left and go through a gate. Walk downhill, passing a house on your right, and go through a gate to reach Afon Arthog. Turn left and pass the bridge you crossed earlier. Stay on the track and follow it uphill to a gate and lane where you join the shorter walk.

9. Turn right along the lane. Pass above a farm and go through a gate across the lane. Follow it downhill through woodlands to the main road. Turn right then go left along the lane to the car park at the start.

Penmaenpool

Route:	This walk starts by following the old railway track beside Afon Mawddach. After this level stretch, the route climbs gradually into the hills, from where there are superb views.
Start:	Car park near the toll bridge and old signal box at Penmaenpool.
Access:	Penmaenpool is on the A493, west of Dolgellau. Buses from Dolgellau Machynlleth and Aberystwyth.
Facilities:	Refreshments at the George 111 Hotel. Picnic tables near the car park and at various places alongside the old railway track. Toilets at the car park.
Maps:	Ordnance Survey Explorer OL23; Landranger 124.

This lovely walk starts by following an easy, level stretch of the Mawddach Trail, a walking and cycling route from Barmouth to Dolgellau. It follows the trackbed of the Ruabon-Barmouth railway line which closed in 1965 after operating for one hundred years. It opened to bring Victorian visitors to the Cambrian coast and transported slate and copper from the local quarries.

The George 111 Hotel at Penmaenpool dates from the mid 17th century when it was an inn and ships` chandlers. Many boats were built on Afon Mawddach, using timber from the nearby oak woods. This stopped on the coming of the railways. When the toll bridge was built in 1979, it could be opened to allow the passage of ships.

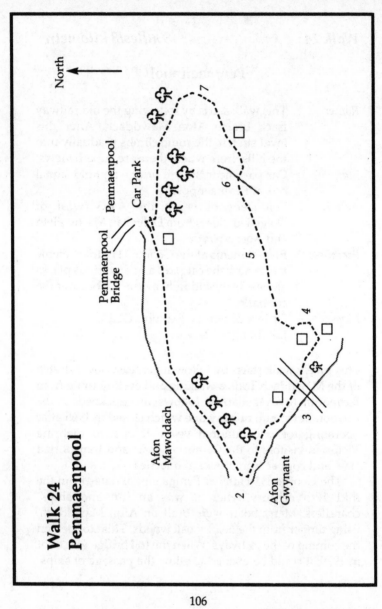

Walk 24
Penmaenpool

North

7

Penmaenpool

Car Park

Penmaenpool
Bridge

6

5

4

Afon
Mawddach

2

Afon
Gwynant

3

Many species of birds can be spotted from the track such as heron, cormorant, common sandpiper and red-breasted merganser. It is worthwhile to carry binoculars. From higher sections of the walk there are superb views of the estuary as well as the Aran mountains and Cader Idris range.

Walk directions:

1. From the car park, walk towards the toll bridge and pass the signal box. Continue along the old railway track beside Afon Mawddach, passing the George 111 Hotel. Go through a kissing-gate and continue along the track. Ignore a little gate on the left at picnic tables and walk on beside Abergwynant Woods. Pass more picnic tables on the left and a reedy area, with outcrops behind it, on the left. Ahead of you is a level bridge. A few paces before reaching it, go left on a wide track, passing around a gate.

2. Ignore a track on the left and go ahead with a small river on your right. Further on, there is a field to your right. When the track veers right, go through a gate into the field and follow the track to another gate where it meets a drive coming from a house on the left. Go ahead, with Afon Gwynant on your right, and ignore a bridge across it. Pass Abergwynant Farm and walk along the lane, through tall trees, to the A493.

3. Cross the road with care. Turn left, then right along a lane. Follow it around bends uphill with views of a ravine below on the right. Pass trees, then a field, on your left. When the field ends, go left on a track, passing a house on your right. When the main track bends left to a house, leave it to go ahead on another track to a gate. To the left of it there is a ladder stile.

4. Follow the track around bends, uphill, pausing now and again to look back at the views. Further on, you will have a wall on the left. Continue along the track and pass a scree covered hill on your right. After the end of the scree, and before the track reaches a wall corner, go left a few paces on a narrow path to a stone step stile in a wall. It has a post with a yellow arrow on it.

5. Go slightly left and over a rise then downhill. The path veers to the left to pass another scree covered hill and wall on the right. Ignore a small gate and follow a fence on the right to a ladder stile. Continue downhill along the right side of the field, passing trees. Go through a gap into the next field, to bear right over a stream.

6. Go ahead on a grassy track with great views of the surrounding mountains. When the track reaches a tree a few metres before a stone building, go left downhill and go through a right-hand gate near farm buildings. Pass a stone building on your right, then go left through a gate and follow a track to a gate and stile. The track heads towards a building, passes it on the left and then winds downhill with a wood on the left, before slanting right to join another track coming from a house.

7. Turn left and, when the track bends right, leave it to go ahead through trees to a ladder stile. Descend the narrow path through scrub and small trees to emerge on a track near a pond. Turn left and ignore a gate and track on the right. Just before reaching a house, go through a gate on the right with a yellow arrow. Pass the side of the house on your left and follow the path downhill to the A493. Cross with care and turn right to the car park and start of the walk.

Bala

Route: This easy, level walk goes along the shoreline of Llyn Tegid and follows embankments beside Afon Dyfrdwy and Afon Tryweryn to Pont y Bala. It then returns through the town, passing the mound of an ancient castle.

Start: Car park at Llyn Tegid, off the A494.

Access: Bala is on the A494, which leaves the A5 at Corwen.Buses from Barmouth, Chester and Wrexham.

Facilities: Full facilities in Bala. Public toilets at the car park and on the walk.

Maps: Ordnance Survey Explorer OL23; Landranger 125.

Llyn Tegid is the longest, natural lake in Wales. This four mile long body of water is associated with many legends and, according to one, a cruel prince called Tegid Foel once ruled the area. One evening, during a feast, he was punished by his palace and its surrounding area being drowned to form the lake. The only survivor was a local harpist who followed a small, singing bird into the mountains. One other story tells how a guard forgot to replace the lid on a spring and its waters flooded the town and valley.

The lake is home to the gwyniad, a member of the herring family, which has been trapped here since the Ice Age. It is not found anywhere else in Britain. Many different kinds of birds visit the lake, including ducks,

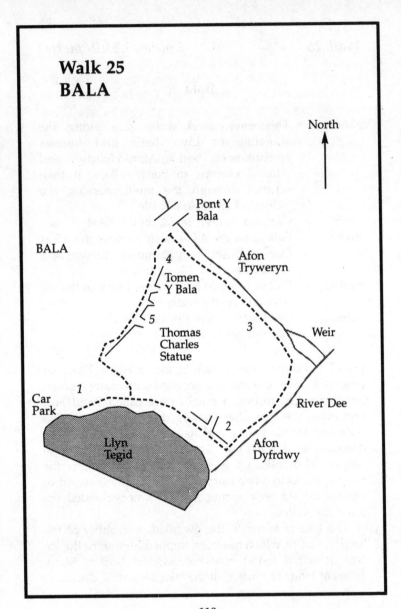

Walk 25
BALA

North

Pont Y
Bala

BALA

Afon
Trywateryn

4

Tomen
Y Bala

5

Weir

Thomas
Charles
Statue

3

Car
Park

1

River Dee

2

Afon
Dyfrdwy

Llyn
Tegid

waders and heron.

Afon Dyfrdwy (River Dee) enters the lake at Llanuwchllyn and it is said the river flows through the lake without mixing with the lake`s waters. Further on in the walk you pass beside Afon Tryweryn which flows from Llyn Celyn, a reservoir which was created in the 1960s to provide water for Liverpool. In spite of many protests, the Welsh speaking community of Capel Celyn, consisting of a school, cottages and farms, were drowned to form the reservoir. The river is now known for its canoeing and white water rafting.

On the walk you pass by Tomen y Bala. This earthwork is about thirty feet high and is thought to date from about the 11th century AD, before an English borough was established. A short diversion of a few metres leads to the statue of Thomas Charles who came to Bala in 1784 and promoted Sunday Schools. Mary Jones of Llanfihangel-y-pennant walked over twenty miles barefoot to Bala in 1800 to purchase one of his Bibles. Impressed by her fortitude, he helped found the British and Foreign Bible Society.

Walk directions:

1. At the car park, have Llyn Tegid (Bala Lake) on your right. Walk through the car park and, at its far end, continue along a path. Follow it to benches at a road. Turn right and ignore a road on the left.

2. After a few more metres, go left at a footpath signpost and pass through a metal kissing-gate. Follow a broad path along an embankment with Afon Dyfrdwy (River Dee) on your right. The path bends left away from the river and passes a weir on Afon Tryweryn. Emerge on a track and cross it to a kissing-gate.

3. Follow an embankment past another weir. Just before a kissing-gate, look to your left across a car park to the prominent mound of Tomen y Bala. Go through the kissing-gate and walk up to a road.

4. Turn left and cross over a road. At the next road, turn left on a road that soon bears right and passes Tomen y Bala on the left. Pass a chapel and at a crossroads go left for about 40 metres to a square, where you will see the statue of Thomas Charles.

5. Return to the crossroads and turn left, passing the Heritage Centre. At the far end of a car park, go left and soon right on a path. It passes behind houses and has fields on the right. At a corner, go through a small gate on the right and follow the right-hand fence to another gate. Turn right along the surfaced path to the car park at the start of the walk.

Tywyn

Route: This walk is almost completely level. After
                following the seafront promenade, the route
                heads through the old airfield to Broad
                Water and Afon Dysynni. On the return, you
                pass St Cadfan`s Church with its ancient
                inscribed stone and the Tal-y-llyn Railway
                Tywyn Station, where there is a railway
                museum.

Start: Tywyn seafront car park

Access: Tywyn is on the A493, west of Machynlleth.
                The resort is on the Machynlleth-Pwllheli
                Cambrian Coast railway line. Buses from
                Aberystwyth, Machynlleth and Dolgellau.

Facilities: Plenty of refreshment places in Tywyn.
                Public toilets on the seafront near the start
                and near the church. Children`s playground
                on the route.

Maps: Ordnance Survey Ol23; Landranger 135.

Tywyn is a quiet seaside resort surrounded by flat land
and a short distance from the sea. After following the
seafront promenade, the walk passes through the old
RAF Tywyn airfield which opened in 1940 and provided
air target training facilities. In 1943, it became No 631
Squadron but, because of problems with winter flooding,
the squadron was moved to Llanbedr in 1945.

From the lakeside of Broad Water are wide views of
the nearby hills. Cormorants may be seen flying along the
Dysynni Valley to Craig y Deryn (Bird Rock) where they

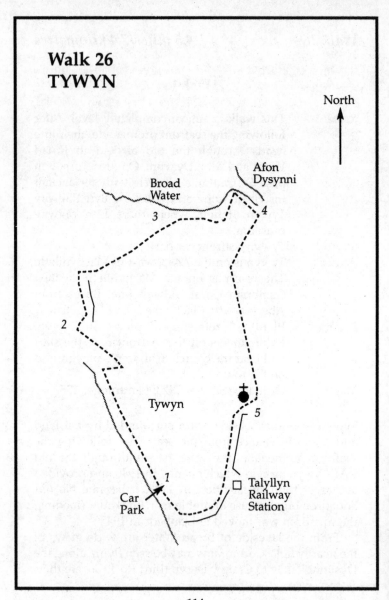

Walk 26
TYWYN

North

Afon
Dysynni

Broad
Water

3

4

2

Tywyn

5

Car
Park

1

Talyllyn
Railway
Station

nest. Birds such as swans, heron, mallard and oystercatcher may be spotted on Broad Water.

On the return route, you pass St Cadfan's Church which was founded in the 6th century. St Cadfan came here on a missionary from Brittany. The first church was burnt down by Vikings and the present building dates from the 12th century. Inside is the Cadfan Stone with its 5th to 7th century inscriptions. They are thought to be the oldest examples of the Welsh language. In the church is an effigy known as the Crying Knight because of the wetness around his eyes in wet weather.

The walk passes the Tal-y-llyn Railway Tywyn Wharf Station where there is a café, a souvenir shop and a small museum with old locomotives. The railway originated from the need to transport slate from the Bryneglwys quarry near Aberynolwyn to the coast. It closed in 1950 but a year later the Tal-y-llyn Preservation Society was formed, the first of its kind.

Walk directions:

1. At the seafront, walk along the promenade with the sea on your left. When the road bends right, continue along the promenade and pass a caravan park on the right. At the end of houses, turn right up to a road and follow it past caravans and over a level crossing. Turn left on another road, and pass a children's playground on the right.

2. After the last of the houses, turn right along a track and follow it to gates. Follow the track as it bears left and continue along it to a fence on an embankment. At a tall pole go left for a few metes then turn right to climb a stile and cross a footbridge over a channel. On reaching open ground, bear right for about 200 metres then slant left in

the direction of Broad Water. The path passes through gorse as you near the lake.

3. Continue beside the lake and along an embankment with the lake on your left and a marshy area on your right. Climb a stile at a broad gate across the track and bear left. The embankment bends right at the point where the lake enters Afon Dysynni. Continue along the embankment and pass under overhead cables and, before the river bends left, look for a footpath signpost. Turn right here into a field.

4. Walk straight ahead with gorse bushes on your left and go ahead through a gap into the next field. Slant left towards a footpath signpost near gates and, when you reach it, bear left through gates and across a level bridge over a channel. Ignore a footbridge on the right and continue along the track beside a fence. Go through a gate across the track and follow a lane, bordered by channels. Pass houses and emerge on the main road near St Cadfan`s Church.

5. Bear right to pass the church on your right. Pass the Old Market Hall and the English Presbyterian Church. Further along on your left, at a road junction, is a memorial to those who died in Africa 1900 – 1901. Here turn left and follow the road past the library and school. On reaching a crossroads, pass the Tal-y-llyn Railway Station on your left and cross a bridge over the main railway line. Continue along the road, ignoring roads off, to the seafront and start of the walk.

Llyn Barfog

Route: This walk makes an ascent of about 400 feet
                to the hillside lake, Llyn Barfog then returns
                past the legendary stone Carn March Arthur,
                with superb views over Afon Dyfi. Part of
                the descent is quite steep and stony.

Start: Snowdonia National Park car park in Cwm
                Maethlon.

Access: From the A493, between Tywyn and
                Aberdyfi, take the road signposted Cwm
                Maethlon (Happy Valley). Alternatively,
                leave the A493 at Cwrt, west of Machynlleth.

Facilities: Full facilities in Tywyn and Aberdyfi.

Maps: Ordnance Survey Explorer OL23:
                Landranger 135.

Llyn Barfog , the Bearded Lake, is covered with water
lilies during the early summer and it is from them that the
name may be derived. According to one legend, a large,
hairy monster once lived in the lake`s waters, but you are
unlikely to see it now because King Arthur caught the
creature and dragged it all the way to Llyn Cau below
Cader Idris. Llyn Barfog is said to be the home of Gwyn
ap Nudd, the king of the fairies and, many years ago,
fairies dressed in green used to walk beside the lake
whilst looking after their white cattle. One of the cows
was caught by a local farmer and she produced lots of
milk and gave birth to many calves. When the cow was
old, the farmer decided to slaughter her but, when the
butcher came, a fairy appeared and called the cow. The

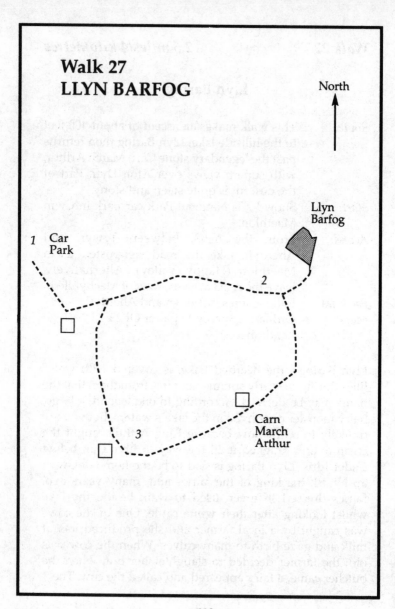

Walk 27
LLYN BARFOG

North

Llyn
Barfog

1 Car
Park

2

3

Carn
March
Arthur

cow and all the cattle descended from her crossed the hill and disappeared into the lake and were never seen again.

Look out for the stone inscribed Carn March Arthur. Beside it is a rock with a hollow that looks like the impression of a horse`s hoof. It is said to be the print left by King Arthur`s horse when it jumped over Afon Dyfi to escape enemies pursuing King Arthur.

Walk directions:

1. From the end of the car park, go through a kissing-gate in the corner and turn left on a track. It goes around bends and passes between farm buildings and a farm house, then goes up to a ladder stile at a gate. Continue uphill along the track, climbing stiles at two gates. Walk through moorland and when the track bears left, maintain your direction to a gate and stile.

2. On your left is Llyn Barfog. Continue on the grassy path that rises to the right away from the lake. Follow it over the hill and keep ahead with a hill on your right. On meeting a fence, bear right to a gate and stile. On your left are views of Afon Dyfi. Just before reaching a wall on your left is the low inscribed stone (Carn March Arthur). Follow the track to a stile and gate and continue descending to gates at a footpath signpost near a house.

3. Turn right on a track behind the house and follow it downhill, passing through a gate. It becomes steeper and stonier before veering to the right of farm buildings to emerge on the track used earlier on the walk. Turn left to retrace your steps past the farm to the car park.

Llanfihangel-y-pennant

Route: On this walk you will have beautiful views
of the Dysynni Valley and Craig y Derwyn
(Birds` Rock). You can visit one of the
strongholds of the Welsh princes and the
site of the cottage where the famous Mary
Jones was born. In the year 1800, she walked
barefoot to Bala to buy a Bible.

Start: Small car park opposite Llanfihangel-y-
pennant church.

Access: From the B4405 at Abergynolwyn, follow the
sign for Castel y Bere. Continue past the
castle`s small car park to the car park
opposite the church. Alternatively, from the
A493 on the coast, lanes can be followed
from Bryncrug and Llanegryn to
Llanfihangel-y-pennant.

Facilities: Toilets at the car park. Refreshments at
Abergynolwyn.

Maps: Ordnance Survey OL23; Landranger 124.

Castell y Bere is only a short diversion from the walk and
is well worth exploring. The castle was built by Llywelyn
ap Iorwerth (Llywelyn the Great) in 1221. His grandson
Llywelyn ap Gruffudd was killed in 1282 by the English
and they took the castle in 1283 and established an
English garrison. Madog ap Llywelyn captured the castle
for the Welsh in 1294, but since then the stronghold does
not appear to have been maintained.

After following lanes and the path below the craggy

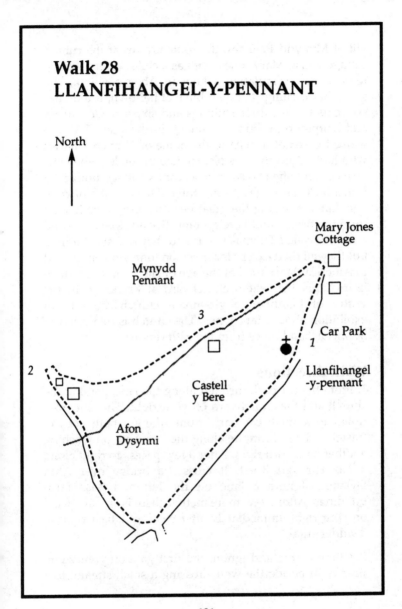

Walk 28
LLANFIHANGEL-Y-PENNANT

North

Mary Jones
Cottage

Mynydd
Pennant

3

Car Park

Llanfihangel
-y-pennant

1

2

Castell
y Bere

Afon
Dysynni

hill of Mynydd Pennant, the route arrives at the ruined cottage where Mary Jones lived as a child. After learning to read at a circulating school in Abergynolwyn, she saved her earnings to buy a Bible of her own. It took her six years to save three shillings and sixpence (seventeen and halfpence in today's money). In the year 1800, she walked barefoot to Bala to the home of Thomas Charles who had set up the schools. He had no Bibles when she arrived, and she stayed in a servant's cottage until they came. Mr Charles gave Mary three Bibles for the price of one. Later, realising the great need for Bibles, he helped form the British and Foreign Bible Society. Mary married a weaver called Thomas Lewis and they had six children, but they all died except for their son John who emigrated to America. Mary died at the age of eighty and her grave is in Capel Bethlehem churchyard at Bryncrug. In the vestry of Llanfihangel-y-pennant church there is an exhibition about Mary Jones. The church is dedicated to St Michael and dates from the 12th century.

Walk directions:

1. From the car park turn left along the lane, passing the church and the churchyard on your right. The lane goes uphill to a small car park, from where a path goes to Castell y Bere. Continue along the lane and, on reaching another lane, turn right. After a few paces, go right along a No Through Road. It crosses a bridge over Afon Dysynni. Ignore a lane on the left and pass farm buildings. After a few more metres, there is an old chapel on your right. Immediately after passing it, bear right to a ladder stile.

2. Climb a stile and ignore the first gate on your right. Bear right beside the wall, crossing a small stream, to a

stile at the next gate. Bear right and climb another stile then continue along the hillside soon getting closer to the right-hand wall. There are a few more stiles to climb, whilst the path continues between the wall and a craggy hillside on your left. Ignore a gate into a field and go through a gate across the path. Pass farm buildings and a flat bridge on your right.

3. Follow a fence and the river now nearby on your right. In a corner, climb a stile and continue beside a fence to the next stile. Follow a track below a house to a gate and lane. Opposite is the site of Mary Jones Cottage. Turn right along the lane to the start of the walk at the car park.